RELEASING THE
P WER
OF THE SMALLER CHURCH

edited by
SHAWN McMULLEN

RELEASING THE P⚡WER

OF THE SMALLER CHURCH

edited by

SHAWN MᴄMULLEN

Cover design by Ross Design

Inside design by Anita Cook

Library of Congress Cataloging-in-Publication Data

Releasing the power of the smaller church / edited by Shawn McMullen.
   p. cm.
   ISBN 978-0-7847-2146-9 (pbk.)
   1. Small churches. 2. Church growth. 3. Church work. I. McMullen, Shawn A.

BV637.8.R45 2007
253--dc22

   2007010456

Published by Standard Publishing, Cincinnati, Ohio. www.Standardpub.com

12 11 10 09 08 07   7 6 5 4 3 2 1

ISBN 978-0-7847-2146-9

DEDICATIONS

To my parents-in-law, Herb and Lois Bleakney,
whose personal lives, marriage, and family
revolved for decades around their service to the smaller church.
"We continually remember before our God and Father
your work produced by faith, your labor prompted by love,
and your endurance inspired by hope in our Lord Jesus Christ"
(1 Thessalonians 1:3).

To leaders and volunteers in smaller churches everywhere
who serve the Lord and his people with joy and gladness.
"Whatever you do, work at it with all your heart,
as working for the Lord, not for men,
since you know that you will receive an inheritance from the Lord
as a reward. It is the Lord Christ you are serving"
(Colossians 3:23, 24).

Together we're making a difference.

TABLE OF CONTENTS

FOREWORD

by Dr. David Faust
Executive Editor, *The Lookout*
President, Cincinnati Christian University
Cincinnati, Ohio

I grew up on a farm in southern Ohio, and my wife grew up in New York City. When we started dating, she would visit our farm. As we walked by the barn, she would turn up her nose and say, "Oooo, what's that *smell?*" My dad would pass by after feeding the hogs, kick off his boots, and say, "Smells like money to me!"

Then I'd visit Candy in the city and we would drive behind a big bus spewing out black smoke from its exhaust pipe. I'd say, "Oooo, what's that *smell?*" Candy would laugh because she understood my point: No matter where you live, something stinks!

In time, both of us discovered the flip side as well. Candy learned to enjoy the sweet fragrance of hay curing in the summer sun and the enticing aroma of my mom's blackberry cobbler cooling on the kitchen counter. I learned to appreciate the smell of fresh bagels and pizza made by ethnic families who had lived in New York for generations.

Truth is, no matter where you serve the Lord or what kind of ministry you fulfill in the church, you can find something undesirable about it. And whether you serve in a big church, a small church, or something in between, you also can find some really sweet things about serving Jesus there. Eugene Peterson is right when he says that "the kingdom is equal parts mystery and mess." The trick is to keep focusing on the mystery.

Jesus taught us to see the enormous potential in a mustard seed. The book of Acts shows there's even greater potential in a small group of disciples who are committed to the Lord and empowered by the Holy Spirit.

There's nothing small about the incredible grace I have experienced in "smaller" churches over the years. The Sunday school teachers who taught me God's Word when I was a boy—they are big in my eyes. So are the preachers who spoke the truth from the pulpit and privately encouraged my walk with the Lord. So are the elders who ordained me, and the faithful brothers and sisters in that healthy rural church who continue to pray for me to this day.

Churches we incorrectly label "small" are filled with potential to reach the lost, equip the saved, and send Christian workers to the ends of the earth. For this I am deeply grateful. And I am grateful to Shawn McMullen and the other authors of this book. Thank you, Shawn, for helping us find the mystery of the power of God amid this marvelous mess we call ministry.

FOREWORD

by Jeff Walling, Minister
Providence Road Church of Christ,
Charlotte, NC

Forgive me, please!

Forgive me for forgetting the power, beauty, and presence of God that is evident in a small gathering of believers in Jesus who mingle their lives in the thing we call church. In the day of megamalls and megachurches, it is easy to forget how important this consistent, stable tool of God truly is. As one writer put it, "God must love smaller churches because he made so many of them!"

As a minister and the son of a minister, I have served and lived in churches both large and small. My first preaching experience was for a smaller church in southern California just down the road from the huge glass chapel known as the Crystal Cathedral. I remember thinking that if we could ever build a church like that, we would have arrived!

Forgive me again. How wrong I was. The power to change the world—the power to draw the hungry and lonely into community with the God who loves them so much he would rather die than live in eternity without them—is not found in grand structures and huge crowds. It is found most vitally in a group of believers who know one another. Who love one another. And who, because of these two key factors, actively care for one another.

And there are the twin blessings of the smaller church on which Shawn McMullen shines the light of truth so effectively in this fine book, *Releasing the Power of the Smaller Church.*

It is a place to truly know others. Only through engagement with other believers in a safe place where one can get past the surface concerns of life and get to the real issues that matter can I ever really say, "I know you."

It happens naturally in the family: You can't eat dinner together with four or five folks for twenty years without finding out who loves lima beans and who won't touch them. So within the smaller church community, relationships of depth and stability are built over time spent with a few.

It is a place to truly care for others. I love America! But to say I truly love each of the 300 million people in this country is ridiculous. Many would rightly say, "How can you say you love me when you didn't even call when my father died?" "How can you say you love me when you've never lifted a finger to help me with my needs or celebrate my victories?" It is in a small community of Christians that I can be the hands and feet of Jesus most effectively.

While small group ministries in larger churches strive to achieve the closeness and depth of relationship we all seek, it happens most naturally in the kind of churches Shawn seeks to serve through this helpful book.

So after you forgive me, dig into these insightful pages and rediscover that there is nothing small about the power and wonder of smaller churches.

ACKNOWLEDGEMENTS

I'm grateful to God for the leaders and volunteers in smaller churches who contributed to this volume. Their love for the Lord and devotion to his church shine through every chapter and page.

I'm grateful to Sheryl Overstreet, administrative assistant for *The Lookout*, who painstakingly produced draft after draft of this book during the editing process. Her willingness to assume the extra work and her dedication to her task helped make this project a joy and not a burden.

I'm thankful for the Energizing Smaller Churches Network (www.escnetwork.org) and the role it plays in bringing value and vision to smaller churches across America. I'm particularly thankful for the visionary men who joined me in creating the network—Dr. David Roadcup, Richard Crabtree, and Brian Lakin—and for those who came aboard early in the process—Shelley Weiss, Jerry Osman, Dr. Joe Ellis, Dr. Bill Bravard, and Mark Taylor—with whom we have worked closely to plan and promote our annual conferences for smaller churches. I'm thankful as well to Kenny and Janice Sanders who graciously volunteered their time to assist us in our first conference season.

I'm thankful to my congregation, the Church of Christ in Milan, Indiana, for allowing me to be their preacher these last eight years. It has been my honor and privilege to serve the Lord in this community with such a wonderful group of Christians. God has blessed us richly, and we're just getting started!

Finally, I'm thankful to my wife Ree, and to our daughters, Kendra, Kyla, and Kelsey, for the love, support, and encouragement God has allowed us to share as a family. Throughout our years together they have helped make the ministry the joy and privilege it is to me.

A NOTE FROM THE EDITOR

This book and its companion volume, *Unleashing the Potential of the Smaller Church* (Standard Publishing, 2006), have grown out of the ministry of the Energizing Smaller Churches Network (www.escnetwork.org).

The ESCN was formed in the fall of 2004 by a group of Christian leaders who share a burden for the ministry of smaller churches (churches with an average Sunday worship attendance of 200 or less). Its goal is to strengthen smaller churches by affirming their value and enlarging their vision. In addition to the annual conferences the ESCN sponsors, plans are underway to make the ESCN a resource center for leaders and volunteers in smaller churches providing audio and print materials, networking opportunities, online dialogue, and consulting connections. Recently the ESCN entered into a formal partnership with Standard Publishing, broadening the organization's influence and opening doors for new ministry opportunities.

As I travel across the country speaking to leaders and volunteers in smaller churches, one comment I often hear goes something like this: "I'm so glad someone is finally doing something for those of us in smaller churches!" In fairness we must acknowledge that churches, individuals, organizations, and Web sites *have been* promoting the ministry of the smaller church long before the ESCN appeared on the horizon. We owe a great debt of gratitude to those who have faithfully fulfilled their calling and paved the way for this ministry. Still for many, the perception is that little is being done to assist and encourage smaller churches in their work. The ESCN prayerfully hopes to alter that perception.

As the minister of a smaller church in Milan, Indiana—home of the 1954 Indiana state basketball champions and inspiration for the acclaimed sports movie *Hoosiers*—I can attest that big things can happen in small places. That's what this book is all about. The chapters you'll read here highlight successful ministries in smaller churches all across America. They show that even with limited personnel and resources, life-changing ministry can happen in the smallest of congregations.

If you serve a smaller church, I pray you will be inspired by what you read and encouraged to put into practice the principles contained in these pages. May God bless you as you do.

CHAPTER ONE

THE POWER
OF THE SMALLER CHURCH

SHAWN MCMULLEN

T HE CHURCH TODAY STANDS AT A CRUCIAL JUNCTURE. Of course many good things are happening in the body of Christ. Megachurches are having a significant impact in metropolitan areas. New and vibrant congregations are being planted all across the country. But for all the good we see, there's much work to be done. Consider these statistics I ran across recently in several church-related Web sites:

- Nearly eighty-five percent of all churches in America are plateaued or declining.
- Half of all churches in America have not added a single new member through conversion growth in the last year.
- Not a single county in America has seen even a one percent increase in church attendance in the last ten years.
- Every year in America, nearly 4,000 churches close their doors.

That's not all:

- Thirty years ago, forty-four percent of Americans were classified as "unchurched." Today that number is closer to sixty-five percent.
- In the last 15 years the number of adults in the U.S. who do not attend church has nearly doubled.
- Altogether nearly 200 million Americans do not have a personal relationship with Christ, making the U.S. the third largest mission field in the world.

It doesn't take an expert to sense the urgency. This is a crucial time for the American church, a time to rise up and impact its culture. And since the majority of churches in America are smaller churches (churches with an average worship attendance of 200 or below), this urgency should be felt keenly by those of us who serve and lead smaller churches. If the spiritual landscape of our nation is to change, smaller churches all across the country will need to play a major role in the process.

But before we consider the potential impact of the smaller church on America's spiritual landscape, let's take a moment to sharpen our perspective.

Small, Medium, or Large

We're drawn to big things: big companies, big schools, big events, and of course, big churches. It isn't wrong to be big, and in fact an organization's "bigness" is often a sign of its health and effectiveness.

But when it comes to churches, the bigness factor can be misleading. Healthy, vibrant, smaller churches exist all across America. These churches are exalting God and transforming their communities. And many other smaller churches across the country have the potential to become healthy and vibrant and to transform their communities for Christ—even though they may never become large or even mid-size congregations.

When it comes to healthy churches, size isn't the only standard of success. God doesn't work that way. If he did, I doubt Jesus ever would have drawn attention to the poor widow who dropped two copper coins into the temple treasury. And I doubt God ever would have asked the prophet Zechariah, "Who despises the day of small things?" (Zechariah 4:10).

Bigger can be good; but so can smaller. As a preacher of a smaller church, I can attest to that. I serve a smaller church in a semi-rural community in southeastern Indiana. We're not large by most standards, but we're healthy. We're maturing in our love for God, his Word, and each other. We're known in our community as a church that helps people. And we're growing.

Shared Victories

There was a time when I looked longingly at the attendance figures and financial reports of larger churches, believing these statistics were the primary indicators of success in ministry. I think differently today. I'm grateful for the ministries of larger churches. We need them. The kingdom needs them. But I've also come to realize that whether our churches are smaller, mid-size, or larger, we're all on the same team and a victory achieved by one church—regardless of its size—is a victory shared by every church.

When an unbeliever responds to the gospel in a smaller church, the victory is shared by every congregation in the body of Christ, including the largest of churches. When a sinner comes to faith in a larger church, that victory too is shared by every congregation in the body of Christ, including the smallest of churches. We may not be aware of every victory, but we share each one because we're working on the same side, supporting the same team, serving the same Lord.

Understanding this simple principle protects us from the critical and competitive spirit that sometimes infiltrates churches. We're all in this together, working to advance God's kingdom on earth. And we're called to support and encourage one another in the process. Smaller churches don't need to distrust or criticize larger churches. And larger churches don't need to feel superior to smaller churches. Jesus said it best when he taught, "So you also, when you have done everything you were told to do, should say, 'We are unworthy servants; we have only done our duty'" (Luke 17:10).

God doesn't focus on the size of the church you serve. He's more concerned about your faithfulness and obedience than the dimensions of your building, your average worship attendance, or your annual budget. Besides, when all is said and done, Heaven levels the playing field. When we're in the presence of God for eternity, there will be no distinction between those who have served him in larger churches and those who have served him in smaller churches. To take it a step further, in Heaven those who have served larger churches can't be proud and those who have served smaller churches can't be jealous!

Unique Opportunities

Marketing professionals know one of the most effective ways to sell or promote a product is to highlight its features and benefits; in other words, "What can the product do and how can it benefit me?" We're not here to sell a certain kind of church, but before we think about ways to make ministry in the smaller church more effective, it may be helpful to consider some of the unique opportunities for growth and service inherent in the smaller church.

Smaller churches provide unique opportunities to know and be known. Because we're a smaller church, I know every member of our church personally. I know the parents and I know their children. I know the kids who attend our youth functions, and I know the names of those who have recently visited us. With few exceptions, I can stand at the door after a service and greet everyone I meet by name. Visitors are easily identified in smaller churches, and if the members are warm and friendly to newcomers, they will leave the service wanting to return. As the song from the once-popular TV show *Cheers* reminds us, people like to go "where everybody knows your name."

Smaller churches provide unique opportunities for inter-generational relationships. When I sit at the front of the auditorium and look out on our congregation each Lord's Day, I'm encouraged to see several generations of families gathered together for worship. Whether they sit side-by-side or throughout the auditorium, the presence of three and sometimes four generations of the same family gathered for worship is an encouragement to the entire church. There's nothing wrong with youth activities and age-appropriate worship opportunities. But at the same time, I get a sense of continuity when I see children worshiping and interacting at church with their parents and grandparents. Smaller churches are in a unique position to foster such relationships.

Smaller churches provide unique opportunities to use gifts and talents. I didn't coin the phrase, but in the church I serve we often operate according to the "good enough" principle. It's natural to assume that the talent pool is smaller in smaller churches. As a result, members of smaller churches with average (or even below average) talent often have opportunities to participate in public worship and ministry in ways that would be denied them in larger churches. This doesn't mean we shouldn't strive for excellence in all we do, but it does mean that in the smaller church, a genuine heart and a willingness to serve are often valued above skill level and professional presentation. In addition, folks in smaller churches are notorious for their tolerance. Those who lead and serve even with modest abilities in the smaller church can expect to be loved, accepted, and encouraged.

Smaller churches provide unique opportunities for leadership development. Opportunities to lead and to train leaders abound in the smaller church. Qualified nursery attendants, Bible teachers, worship leaders, youth workers, elders, and deacons are in great demand in the smaller church. Smaller churches that seize such opportunities to recruit, equip, and encourage people to fill these roles will find themselves developing new leaders all the while.

Smaller churches provide unique opportunities for direct contact between the preacher and the people. In smaller churches the proximity of the pulpit to the pew is often greater than in larger churches. This is true literally during the worship service, but it's also true when it comes to personal contact. Preachers in smaller churches are often more accessible to the congregation and able to shepherd the flock of God in some very personal ways. Visitors to smaller churches are more likely to find the preacher in their homes in the weeks following their visit. If you're a member of a smaller church, you're more likely to be visited in the hospital by your preacher rather than another member of the church staff. (That is partly because the preacher may be the only member of the church staff!) A new member of a larger church had a brief stay in a local hospital. When a staff member of the church stopped in to visit, the new member admitted, "I'm glad you came by, but I was hoping the preacher would come and see me." The staff member quipped, "You don't want to be that sick!"

Here's another significant benefit. In the smaller church the preacher is often in a unique position personally to disciple young people. From time to time I hear about or read statistics pointing to a decline in the number of young men entering the preaching ministry. If the statistics are accurate, we should all be concerned. And no one is in a better position to help reverse this trend by recruiting and equipping young men to enter the pulpit ministry than the preacher of the smaller church. I teach a Sunday school class of teenage boys in the church I serve. I look forward to spending time with them in class each week and planning special activities for them. But most of all I enjoy investing a part of my life in their lives on a weekly basis. I'm anticipating that some of the young men in my class will eventually enroll in a Christian college and train for the ministry. This is also why I continue (even as a member of the "over fifty" club) to lead a week of church camp for teenagers every summer. I want to do my part to encourage and equip young men and women for ministry, and rubbing shoulders with them every opportunity I get is part of that strategy.

I haven't done the research, but I'm guessing that if a poll were taken today of preachers, youth workers, missionaries, and other vocational Christian servants, it would reveal that a large percentage of them came from smaller churches where they were discipled by a preacher, Sunday school teacher, or other church leader, and where they had ample opportunity to develop their gifts and passion for ministry.

Smaller churches provide unique opportunities to impact communities. Not all smaller churches are located in small towns. But those that are will find themselves in a unique position to impact their communities. One of the most significant goals any smaller church in a small town can set is to transform the spiritual landscape of its community. Word travels quickly in small towns, and a church can easily develop a positive (or negative) image by its actions. A smaller church that resists community involvement soon finds itself on the periphery of its community. But a congregation that engages its community and assists those who belong to it soon becomes known throughout the town as "the church that cares about people."

A member of our church was talking with a prominent member of our community about food baskets our members were preparing for families in our town. The community member asked, "And what church do you attend?" When our member identified our congregation, her friend observed, "That church is always doing something good!" You can't buy that kind of advertisement.

Speaking of advertisement, smaller churches in small communities often have easier and cheaper access to local media than churches in larger metropolitan regions. When our church advertises in our local paper, we can afford to purchase quarter-page or half-page ads. It's not difficult to get our announcements on local radio either. During a recent spring weekend, our church hosted a group of thirty college students who came to our town as part of a national service project tour. We fed and housed the students, worked side-by-side with them on a number of community service projects, invited members of the community to join us, and honored the students as guests during our Sunday morning worship service. Representatives from two regional newspapers and a local radio station attended the weekend events and responded with several full pages of newspaper coverage and radio interview time. All of which, we believe, made a lasting impact on our community.

Setting the Stage for Growth

Transforming the spiritual landscape of your community is a noble goal, but desire alone will not make it happen. Smaller churches that want to impact their communities for Christ must spend time preparing for that impact. I call this "setting the stage for growth." Knowing that God is the one who causes the church to grow (see Acts 2:47 and Colossians 2:19), we must also realize there are certain things a church can do in partnership with God to assist the growth (see 1 Corinthians 3:9). Churches do this in many ways.

Focus on health. I'm glad to see the emphasis shifting in many Christian circles from church growth to church health. We all know growth is important and numbers represent souls. But as we're hearing more and more today, the health of a church should be its priority with the understanding that growth is a by-product of health.

Health professionals tell us that if we want healthy physical bodies we must choose a certain lifestyle, one that includes a healthful diet, regular exercise, and adequate rest. Acknowledging the value of the lifestyle is a starting point, but that alone won't produce results. We must put the principles of the lifestyle into practice, consciously making daily choices to live the lifestyle we've adopted.

Even then it may take some time before we realize the benefits of the lifestyle. But the lack of instant gratification doesn't (or shouldn't) deter us from achieving our goal. We stay with the program even when we don't see immediate results, trusting that the results will be evident in time.

A similar principle holds true in the church. In a recent leadership meeting in the church I serve, Tom, one of our elders, introduced a series of statistics he had compiled on the growth of our congregation. His charts showed that in the last four years the worship attendance in our smaller church had doubled, and in the last six years our offerings had nearly tripled. We were encouraged by the statistics, but to me the most significant aspect of Tom's report was its element of surprise. Because these increases occurred steadily and incrementally over the last several years, I hadn't given a great deal of thought to them. It wasn't until someone put it down on paper that I saw the true extent of the growth God has given us. We had been focusing on the health of our congregation during those years, and our growth stemmed from the health we attained.

Focus on truth. The faithful preaching and teaching of biblical truth is of paramount importance to every church. Upholding Scripture as the divinely inspired Word of God and challenging believers to conform to its holy standard are keys to church health and growth.

The apostle John wrote, "It gave me great joy to have some brothers come and tell about your faithfulness to the truth and how you continue to walk in the truth. I have no greater joy than to hear that my children are walking in the truth" (3 John 3, 4). Paul wrote to Titus, "You must teach what is in accord with sound doctrine" (Titus 2:1) and to Timothy, "Watch your life and doctrine closely. Persevere in them, because if you do, you will save both yourself and your hearers" (1 Timothy 4:16).

I'm not presenting this as new information, but as a reminder that programs and activities are no substitutes for the simple proclamation of the truth. Whatever else you do to help your smaller church reach people, make sure the foundational truths of Scripture (the gospel plan of salvation, the nature of the church, the nature of life in Christ, and so on) remain front and center.

Focus on fruit. Setting the stage for growth requires an emphasis on the Christian lifestyle as well. Sound doctrine is vital to the life of the church. But so is Christian living. One is not more important than the other.

Have you ever known someone who had been a member of a church for decades, who had listened to thousands of sermons and participated in thousands of Sunday school lessons and Bible studies, whose life still did not bear the fruit of the Spirit (Galatians 5:22, 23)? Honestly—how can someone hear all that teaching for all those years and still be crotchety, critical, mean-spirited, or prone to gossip? People like that have failed to examine themselves in light of Scripture.

It's unfortunate when this happens, but we can't leave it at that. Any church wanting to prepare itself for growth and impact in its community must do all it can to ensure that its members are living the Christian lifestyle—and in ways that are easily identified by others. Paul was clear about his objective for the church: "We proclaim him, admonishing and teaching everyone with all wisdom, so that we may present everyone perfect in Christ. To this end I labor, struggling with all his energy, which so powerfully works in me" (Colossians 1:28, 29). It seems Paul wasn't willing to settle for anything less than a church where every member was perfect (that is, mature or complete) in Christ.

Granted, much of this is beyond the control of any person or group. Still, one of the primary responsibilities of any church is to help its members become more and more like Christ. And it begins with the leadership. Nineteenth-century Scottish preacher Robert Murray McCheyne noted, "My people's greatest need is my personal holiness." An emphasis on holiness in the lives of the preacher, elders, and other leaders will go a long way to encourage holiness in the lives of the congregation.

I've learned a great deal from the sermons I've preached through the years, but without question a series I preached on Jesus' Sermon on the Mount (Matthew 5–7) has been the most significant and life changing for me. By the time I completed the series (a total of 32 messages), I had examined my life in light of Scripture like I never had before. Many people in our church made similar comments about the effect the series had on their lives.

The transformation of the lives of church members is vital not only because it's a matter of obedience to Christ, but because it represents the most effective evangelistic tool a church possesses. Outsiders are drawn to the gospel when they notice that the lives of Christians are truly different from those who don't know Christ.

Focus on unity. "Make every effort to keep the unity of the Spirit through the bond of peace," wrote the apostle Paul in Ephesians 4:3. This command holds true for every congregation, but it has special significance for smaller churches seeking to transform the spiritual landscape of their communities. Many larger congregations have a well-defined leadership team, and most members of these churches understand how and by whom decisions are made. This isn't always true in smaller churches. The unique dynamics of the smaller church often mean that decisions are made by a number of different people in a number of different positions.

Because one or two dissenting voices can make a big difference in a smaller church, it's important that the members of smaller churches understand and value the biblical concept of unity. In an attempt to do what larger churches are doing, some leaders of smaller churches may move too quickly to implement change, alienating and even losing members in the process. This isn't entirely unavoidable, but in many cases it can be prevented. When a church understands that Christian unity is as important as any other biblical doctrine, and when its people are willing to "make every effort" to preserve unity in the body, even smaller churches can weather the storms of change in ways that honor God.

Focus on prayer. Of all the things a smaller church can do to set the stage for growth and outreach, this is the most important. Yet sadly, it's often the most neglected. It's not that we don't pray—in our worship services and during Bible studies and before fellowship dinners. It's that we seldom give prayer its rightful place in the process of growth and ministry.

If I could recommend a starting point for every smaller church wanting to change the spiritual landscape of its community, it would be to pray—to hold special sessions of prayer focusing specifically on the life, health, ministry, and growth of the church. The church I serve holds a prayer service for this purpose every quarter. Our services correspond with the changing of the seasons, so we call the service "A Season of Prayer." During this time we reflect on the answers to prayer we've seen in our congregation, talk about our goals and objectives for the coming months, and spend time together in prayer, asking God for his blessings and power as we do the work he calls us to do. We pray for unity, for wisdom, and for love in all we undertake.

You may choose to meet for prayer more often. Whatever you choose to do, the important thing is that your church gathers together regularly to seek God's help in ministry. John Wesley said, "God does nothing but in answer to prayer." James explained, "You do not have, because you do not ask God" (James 4:2). Jesus reminded us, "If you remain in me and my words remain in you, ask whatever you wish, and it will be given you" (John 15:7). Make prayer a priority.

Looking Ahead

When it comes to ministry in the smaller church, we've barely scratched the surface. In the chapters that follow you'll learn from leaders across the country whose smaller churches are having a dynamic impact on peoples' lives and changing the spiritual landscape of their communities. These congregations have found ways to release the power that resides within the church. Your church can do the same. Read on.

CHAPTER TWO

PERSONAL GROWTH:
THE LEADER'S WALK WITH GOD

JERRY REEVES

Houston, Texas. Home of millions of people, the Astros, Comets, Rockets, Texans, Johnson Space Center, Mission Control, high humidity, and my church. We are located in the Clear Lake City area where much of the space program resides. Our dream is to communicate the gracious love of God in concrete ways that will draw people into the kingdom. We've been on a long journey together. Eighteen years ago I began working with this church as a youth minister. Twelve years ago I accepted the position of senior minister. We've moved physically, geographically, spiritually, emotionally, and theologically. We are continually overwhelmed that God is at work among us, doing creative things to help us grow into the 21st century.

New Beginnings Church is a fantastic church of around 200 Sunday morning worshipers—we meet inside a huge facility we co-own with a Christian school and daycare. We are honored to have two other magnificent churches meeting in our facility as well. We are seeking to live in the unity Jesus prayed for in John 17.

This year I participated in my first ever 5K run . . . well . . . for me it was a 5K walk. I placed third in my age group at the awards ceremony. Then I found out I was the only one who had entered in my age group! Sometimes that's how people feel when they approach their personal devotional life. They feel as if they would lose the race even if they were the only one entered. And perhaps equally as ridiculous, others mistakenly believe they are doing so well they have nothing to learn.

A Time of Searching

I grew up in a Christian home. My parents raised me "in the church,"

29

which means we were present at every service. While I was in the 10th grade, the little church we attended split over issues that seem small now, but at the time were monumental. As our family sought to find answers, we combed the Scriptures looking for "proofs" to support or put down the competing theologies. As the years passed, the shallowness of this method challenged my faith and changed my life story.

I attended a Christian college and my search continued. I attempted to frame questions that exceeded my vocabulary and could not seem to find the spiritual, cognitive, and emotional answers I needed. I did what most do. I ignored them. For a while I tried to make the questions go away by staying busy or filling my mind with other things. I pursued a career in teaching, thinking the ministry must not be for me. But the questions would not go away.

I moved to Houston to accept a position as a youth minister and found a church in many ways similar to the little church that split in my youth; and yet, in many ways it was quite different. The questions moved again to the forefront of my mind. "Who is this Jesus?" "Is he interested only in my performance?" "What about the Father-son relationship?" "Is Christianity an exercise in intellectual futility, or does it provide something solid to hold onto?" As I reflected on the issues that split our little church, I asked, "Is this what Christ died for? Is this what the martyrs would look back on and say, 'yeah—that's what I died for'?" Surely not!

It was in a graduate class that God began clarifying my questions and providing me with answers. My degree plan called for a class titled "Christian Spiritual Formation." I remember looking at the title and wondering what in the world it meant. In my mind, I had likened it to "underwater basket weaving," a name reserved for courses that are totally useless but still part of the degree plan.

Was I in for a surprise.

I had what I thought was a reasonably well-developed spiritual life. I had read the Scriptures, though not in any orderly fashion. I had prayed my 9-1-1 prayers as well as my 4-1-1 prayers. I attended church and a Bible college. I taught Sunday school. I was on staff as a youth minister. Surely I, of all people, understood spirituality.

But during this classroom experience I learned about a waterless place in my soul that received torrents of nurturing grace. I had never before understood this place, but came to realize this was where my questions originated. Words penetrated my heart and soul that had been available for almost two millennia in devotional writings—writings that were either largely ignored by my spiritual influences or simply not known. I suspect it was the latter.

I recall thinking, "I'm 37 years old! Why has no one told me about this before now?"

An Awakening

One afternoon after class had been dismissed, students around me moved about gathering their things and exiting. All I could do was sit still. I am usually in control of my emotions, but that afternoon I had a lump in my throat. Tears burned in my eyes because of the tender encounter I'd had with my Savior.

It was unmistakable.

As I sat there, my beloved mentor approached and talked with me. He knew he was entering into a holy place with me, a place I had ventured into perhaps for the first time in my life. He spoke carefully and perceptively. I remember confessing to him, "I came here expecting to find academia. I did not expect to be touched at the center of my soul."

It seemed the power of God was breaking me down and building me up at the same time. Paul's statement in Philippians began dawning on me: "that he who began a good work in you will carry it on to completion until the day of Christ Jesus" (Philippians 1:6). God is extremely . . . well . . . *creative* . . . in the way he goes about accomplishing this.

Before, I thought personal devotions were designed to expose my weaknesses in an attempt to increase my self-discipline and make me behave better. I resisted it like I would resist severe discipline. I discovered these disciplines do help me grow in my behavior, but not by severe discipline or guilt. God is the faithful, tender, healer of my soul. His discipline is accurate, purposeful, and immersed in love. He uses my time with him to help me, not to harm me. His plan is to prosper me and give me a hope and a future.

In a world that does not understand grace, the message of grace is the only life-giving answer. Ministers often find themselves in a peculiar light. When they fall into sin, their fall can create a tremor that has the potential to scandalize the message of grace.

In moments when Christ-like, graceful forgiveness needs emphasis, we often fall victim to legalistic, life-sucking judgment that gives the world reason to say, "See, I told you so. The church is no different from the world." It's not that ministers stand above the church with the message of grace, but rather that we journey together with the church, heart to heart, hand in hand, laboring to grow up into this incredible, indescribable gift that is way too big for us, but is ours nonetheless.

Clear Vision

In order to do so, our vision must be clear.

When we view the Bible as a text to be deciphered and God as a power to be feared and appeased, grace cannot do its loving work. Relationship comes through time spent with one another—times where conversation is rapid and full and times when nothing is said, and in either situation, both parties are at ease.

We are not here to set the world right. We are not here to convict the world of sin. (That's the Holy Spirit's job.) We are here to grow in grace like everyone else, but we are given the honor of leading God's precious people into this magnificent grace. The only way we can lead is if we follow the one who leads.

How do we go about that kind of relationship with God who is spirit when we are in the flesh?

Time in the Word

The first place to begin is in the Word. Depending on your familiarity with the Bible, you may find this a difficult place to begin. Familiarity can be as much of a disadvantage as unfamiliarity. I was challenged to journey and pray for God to lead. He is faithful. If you'll do the same, you'll discover he really is new and fresh every morning.

People in our culture are used to looking for truth along a path that illuminates our understanding where we are and where we think we need to go. But Scripture contains truths along the way that are beside us, in front of us, behind us, and available to us, even when we fail to see them. So we must keep revisiting those places, reading again and again, praying for God's wisdom and discernment.

Spending time in the Word has shaped my reading and helped me acknowledge my biases. It lets me see the Bible as more than a rulebook—a law to be interpreted with loopholes to be explored so I can determine what I can get away with and still get into Heaven. Instead, the Bible is becoming more and more the revelation of the extravagance of God's gracious, loving character. The Old Testament is no longer the story of a harsh God intent on venting his wrath by pouring out judgment on a people incapable of satisfying his stringent demands.

Now through the Old Testament God shows me something about myself, revealing the arrogance of fallen humankind and providing a plan to correct this mess we've gotten ourselves into. The Old Testament is like a parent correcting a child in stages in order to achieve the desired result—not a mindless obedience, a cowing down to a greater power for fear of greater punishment, but rather a love that precludes any reason for punishment, any desire for disobedience, any need for rebellion. Without God's Word to guide us, our perverted, distorted hearts focus on the punishment and we fail to see the love.

The New Testament reveals the most stunning act of all. When all else failed and hope seemed lost, God did the unthinkable. He died for us. The magnitude of this priceless gift is revealed in degrees as we embrace the Scripture story as God embraces us through it.

I would never have seen this had I not broken down the text into its smaller parts and put it back together (and had the text break me down into smaller parts and put me back together).

So I read the text personally. It is God's message to humanity, but it is also God's message to me. It is a communal message and an individual message. Cultivating my devotional life allows God's Word to read and interpret me as I read and interpret it.

Devoted to Prayer

Relationships are only as good as the communication that supports them. If the communication is one-sided and selfish, the relationship suffers. God is a listener. He hears the cries of the brokenhearted.

Through prayer, the window of the soul is lifted and the fresh wind of the Holy Spirit flows freely. I came to prayer thinking it was my time to talk; I have since learned the value of coming to prayer with the goal of listening. I do not feel the need to talk all the time. I am comfortable sitting and allowing the Spirit to fill my soul with good things—sometimes the good things come from my surroundings. Sometimes they come by reflecting on my past or present. At times God rebukes me and at times he guides me. I pay close attention. God is the Author of all that is good. I want to follow his lead.

There are many ways to enjoy a rich prayer life. Early risers, night owls, the eloquent, and those who struggle putting thoughts together can commune with God in prayer. Strategy is not a basis for relationship. That's true in our prayer lives too.

A professor of mine once directed my attention to the prayers Paul prayed at the beginning of his letters. To me it was like finding a treasure that had been hidden in a field. Now I take those prayers, change the pronouns, and pray them over my family, my friends, and even myself. Take for an example this passage from Ephesians 1 that I love to pray over my family:

> Ever since I began praying about your faith in the Lord Jesus and the development of your love for all the saints, I have not stopped giving thanks for Kristine, Jordan, Jonathan, and Joel [insert the names of your family member or the focus of your prayer], remembering each one of them in my prayers. I keep asking that the God of our Lord Jesus Christ, the glorious Father, may give them the Spirit of wisdom and revelation, so that they may know him better. I pray also that the eyes of their hearts may be enlightened in order that they may know the hope to which he has called each of them, the riches of his glorious inheritance in the saints, and his incomparably great power for us who believe (based on Ephesians 1:15-20).

The Psalms also are rich with dialogue for prayer. Lament, praise, desperation, encouragement, wisdom, and confession are all found there. Here are a couple of psalms I find close to my heart:

> Search me, O God, and know my heart; test me and know my anxious thoughts. See if there is any offensive way in me, and lead me in the way everlasting (Psalm 139:23, 24).

And

> One thing I ask of the LORD,
> this is what I seek:
> that I may dwell in the house of the LORD
> all the days of my life,
> to gaze upon the beauty of the LORD
> and to seek him in his temple (Psalm 27:4).

Praying the Scriptures centers you and gives you peace and direction. Whether you are walking through the storm and the only prayer you can pray is Peter's, "Lord, save me!" (Matthew 14:30), or if you are hungry and find your voice in one of the psalms or one of Paul's prayers, you will not walk away empty.

Keeping a Journal

This leads me to another discipline—journaling.

Take time to write down your prayers, at least occasionally. For years I journaled on my computer. I am a reasonably quick typist, and I enjoyed inputting and saving my files.

Later I was convicted that I wanted to pass on a legacy of prayer to my sons. I felt they needed to see my own handwriting, not just my own keystrokes. So I bought an inexpensive composition book and began. By the way, I have several of those in different locations so that when I want to journal, I don't have to worry that my journal isn't with me. True, the dates get mixed up, but I'm not worrying about it. I'll let my sons sort it all out someday!

The primary rule when journaling is "there are no rules." I mean it. Spelling does not count; grammar does not count; punctuation does not count. I write or type as fast as I can, and I don't worry about cleaning it up. You can write in pencil or ink—red ink, green ink, or purple ink (a personal favorite of mine). You can even write with a marker or crayon. It doesn't matter. Let your writing be the expression of your heart. My best friend often doodles or draws pictures as he journals. When I try to draw a picture, I get bogged down in the details. So I seldom draw simply because I want to let my prayers flow freely. You may express yourself effectively through art—great! Remember, the purpose is to develop your relationship with God. If detail helps you do that, please proceed. Detail distracts me, so I move on.

Some days I may write several pages and some days I may write only a single sentence. One day I simply wrote, "I just don't feel well today." That was all. Don't worry about writing for quantity or quality; the purpose is to be honest and transparent before God and to let your heart speak and listen.

A word of caution: Be patient. Journaling takes time and effort. Many people live in a culture of dishonesty. "How are you doing?" people ask on the street or even at church. We respond, "Fine," when in reality life is sickening and we really need someone to talk to. Such a facade can drive a wedge between us and others and between us and God, leading us to believe no one is really interested in whether or not we're "fine." When a person is accustomed to the apathetic and impersonal, it takes time and effort to rediscover the personal.

Writing makes us vulnerable. What if someone finds and reads your journal? I am careful with prayers of a sensitive nature that could harm someone. I usually put those on my computer and make the document password protected. In other cases, however, I feel God works best with me when I am feeling vulnerable. My devotional life does not place me in that position; I am already there. My devotional life simply accentuates my vulnerability. It is good to be utterly dependent on the one, true, living God!

I find that I receive many blessings from the time I spend in the Scriptures and through prayer and journaling. I have also learned that when

I am the most constant influence in this equation I am missing something valuable, even critical, to wholesome spiritual development—the influence of the community of faith.

I realize I cannot invite the community of faith into my personal devotional times. My house isn't big enough! So, I extend a different invitation. I bring into my quiet times authors such as Henri J. M. Nouwen, Richard Foster, Dallas Willard, C. S. Lewis, Brother Lawrence, and Rob Bell among others. These writers don't give me watered-down-marketplace-stuff, but rich, soul probing, thought provoking, faith building concepts of hope and grace and truth. It was through these readings that those nagging questions that avoided language and clarity began finding their place and speaking their peace and giving me hope.

Some of these writings come in the form of novels. Others are short pieces designed to aid my reflection. Sometimes the topic presented is dense, and each word seems weighted carefully to communicate meaning on several levels. Sometimes the words seem lighter, intended to bless from the surface without the deep penetration of cognitive recognition. God is faithful. He knows what I need when I need it and he provides.

Getting Started

Whenever I read a chapter like this one that I am writing, I wonder, "How can I get started?" My personality is such that I often try to dive off and attempt everything at once and experience failure so quickly that I abandon the pursuit. Let me recommend that you try one or two things at first. Then add as God directs you.

Let me encourage you to find a specific place of solitude. For some of you that means you have to get up early before the rest of the household is up and stirring. By nature I am not an early morning person. I would be much happier if the day started around 10:00 AM and ended around 1:00 AM. Once when some well-meaning people questioned my spirituality, I succumbed to the regimen of early morning prayer and Bible study. I found it exhilarating and wonderful. Quiet mornings out on our deck, watching the sun rise over the horizon as the Son rose in my heart. Up to that time I had rarely started my day at sunrise. (During college I'd seen plenty of sunrises at the end of my day, but that's another story.) I'd play music, a favorite CD, or my guitar. I'd read my Bible or a devotional book and journal. It was inspiring.

Then, in typical fashion, something would happen—a night would come when the hours got too late and the 5:00 AM wake-up call was too early, and I'd spend my time in devotion to pastor pillow and my own personal warm and inviting congregation of covers. Once I broke the regimen, I found it difficult to establish again.

If you do not have a systematic plan for reading through your Bible, I recommend that you get one. Reading through the Bible systematically allows you to read all of God's Word in a year and protects you from leaving out books or chapters you may not understand or enjoy reading. *The One Year© Bible* is my personal favorite. What I like about this system is that you read portions from the Old Testament, the New Testament, Psalms, and Proverbs each day. Many get bogged down and lose heart when they are reading straight through and get to some of the genealogy passages in the Old Testament. But when you read systematically, even when you are in a particularly dry area or an area that does not immediately speak to you, you know another part is coming.

If you have a reading plan, great! Stick with it. After reading the New International Version of *The One Year© Bible* for a few years, I had a friend challenge me to read a different version. I've enjoyed the *New Living Translation* the past several years.

One drawback to this plan is that you can get so focused on reading the passage for the day that you forget to relax and let the passage read you (work on you). I suggest that you give yourself at least 30 minutes daily for relaxed and careful reading.

I know, where will you get the time?

I have found that when I take this time, God multiplies my time the rest of my day. Most of the time, when I spend time with God—I mean unrushed, focused time with him—the rest of my day goes a little smoother, or perhaps I'm a little smoother for the rest of the day! I still have days where I think I am just too busy to take the time to read, and my experience is that those days tend to be longer, harder, and less peaceful than the others.

Start journaling. Don't put it off. Don't grade your writing. Just write. Think of your journal entries as your personal collection of letters to God. Be honest. Be respectful. Be you. God is big enough to take whatever you can dish out in your times of anger, and he is tender and compassionate enough to deal with your heart when you are wounded deeply. He knows you and he loves you.

Finally, read. Invite the community of faith (specifically others who write about the Christian faith and experience) to speak to your development. Ponder over what they write. One of my favorite authors is Henri J. M. Nouwen. I find his writings particularly insightful for my ministry. One of my favorite books is *The Inner Voice of Love,* (Doubleday, 1996). Nouwen gives the instructions not to read this book cover to cover, but instead to pick and choose. Read a portion, usually only a page long, and let God soak you in it. I've read portions that meant something as I read them, then I walked away and something brought them back to mind and I realized there was more to it for me than I first thought. The next day, I returned to the reading to explore it again because God had ministered to me so powerfully over the course of the previous day.

I cannot close without mentioning that there is a world of spiritual disciplines that are designed to help you grow in your love for the Lord. Richard Foster's fine work, *Celebration of Discipline,* (Harper San Francisco, 1998) lists 12 different disciplines along with suggestions for implementing them. This is perhaps the landmark work of our generation when it comes to exploring the disciplines.

If you have never engaged in these kinds of disciplines, getting started can be difficult. Remember, all you can do is all you can do; but all you can do is enough.

May you share in God's richest blessings and find your voice in the disciplines of the personal devotional life.

CHAPTER THREE

PREACHING AND TEACHING:
FINDING TIME, STAYING FRESH

STEVEN MAHONEY

WELCOME TO NEWARK!

When I tell people I'm from Newark, many people assume I mean Newark, New Jersey. But there is a lesser-known Newark in Delaware. Newark is part of the crowded northern half of the northernmost county in Delaware. It is connected to Wilmington, the largest city in the state, by neighborhoods of tract housing and strip shopping centers. The city of Newark has a permanent population of around 30,000, but the population of New Castle County is over half a million. Newark is home to the University of Delaware, and during the school year the city population nearly doubles.

If you were to exit from Interstate 95 to go to Newark, you would pass a Daimler Chrysler assembly plant before arriving at the university. This provides a sense of the variety in our area as well as the variety found in the Newark Church of Christ. Auto assembly plant workers and college students and teachers live, work, and worship with one another at the Newark Church of Christ. The church is spiritual home to employees of other major employers in the area as well, including Bank of America and DuPont.

The Newark Church of Christ is located two miles south of Main Street. The church building is in a heavily residential area surrounded by single-family homes, town homes, and apartments. It is a transitional area. Many people come and go in both community and church. The church is made up of people with diverse backgrounds. Many members have roots in Churches of Christ and Independent Christian Churches, but there are "first generation" Christians as well.

In the 1970s the church began an outreach to the community through Aletheia Christian School and Day Care. Approximately 250 young people receive Christian education each day through this ministry. The church has a number of teachers in the congregation serving from Aletheia Christian school and other local school districts. In the 1990s the congregation began to work with college students and today the Delaware Christian Campus Ministry Foundation ministers to students through a student center located near the heart of the campus.

Historically, the Newark church emphasized community ministry. For years the congregation offered foster care through a home on the property. Today that house offers short-term stays for families who have loved ones in one of the local hospitals. Our members are also active in providing food and cooking meals for needy people. Overall, the Newark Church of Christ is a diverse, active congregation.

Youthful Enthusiasm

The songbooks were tucked away in the pews. Communion had been served and the trays were neatly stacked in the back of the auditorium. The offering was collected and safely stored in the office. Now all eyes were on the young man ascending the steps to the pulpit. He visited the congregation a few times over the past year when he was in the area to see his family. The congregation hadn't known him long, did not know him well, nor did he know them. They were a small country church, between preachers, and one Sunday he offered to help out. This was his first sermon.

What I said that morning has long been lost. I can't remember the text I used, the points from my outline, or my illustrations. All I remember was that it was eight minutes long and it contained everything I knew. And I was supposed to preach Sunday night as well!

Perhaps my story describes a situation you experienced, either as the speaker or as a hearer. It is the kind of thing that happens in smaller churches. I am sure I brought youthful enthusiasm to the congregation, but I doubt there was much else.

More than a quarter century has passed since my first attempt at preaching. Along the way I transitioned from "filling the pulpit" on occasion to full-time ministry staff to full-time preaching ministry. Just as my journey to the pulpit has taken years and many twists and turns, it has taken me time to recognize the power of preaching and teaching to release the power of God in a congregation.

If you preach and teach in a smaller church, you probably wear many hats. You have one or two sermons to prepare each week. Often you will have a Sunday morning Bible class and a Wednesday evening study as well. In addition, your congregation expects you to visit those who are hospitalized and shut-in, make connection with guests, resolve conflicts, counsel, conduct weddings and funerals, fix the plumbing, vacuum the foyer, prepare the bulletin, and so on. You probably have a family, a few personal interests or hobbies, and you recognize the importance of keeping your own spiritual fire burning brightly. How do you do it all?

The Power of the Pulpit

To release the power of God in the smaller church, start with the pulpit. I came of age as a Christian at a time when small group ministry reigned supreme. For years I focused on small groups, personal Bible studies, visitation, and so on. These are important in the life of the church. But preaching takes place when all or most of the church is gathered. A biblical sermon delivered with passion has power to change many lives.

I have a friend who is an engineer. He likes to speak of "man-hours" (not by any means excluding "woman-hours"). If you have a church of 100 members and you preach for a half an hour, you have used 50 man-hours. Maybe "used" is the wrong word. You have "invested in" 50 man-hours. The time you spend delivering that sermon is the most productive time in your week. At no other time will you have an opportunity to make a difference in so many people's lives.

Paul sought to remind Timothy of the most important aspect of his ministry. While I doubt Paul was speaking of the modern, western concept of time management, he certainly spoke of priorities: "In the presence of God and of Christ Jesus, who will judge the living and the dead, and in view of his appearing and his kingdom, I give you this charge: Preach the Word;

be prepared in season and out of season; correct, rebuke and encourage—with great patience and careful instruction" (2 Timothy 4:1, 2).

I used to spend as much time preparing a Bible class as I did studying for a sermon. Often I would think about or study for a small group lesson longer than my sermon. Sometimes I would even wait until Sunday afternoon to prepare my Sunday evening sermon!

My friend's concept of "man-hours" has changed the way I view my week. Today I block out time to prepare my Sunday morning sermon. I am in "do not disturb" mode a couple of hours every day working on my sermon. I hate to admit it because I want to be excellent in everything I do, but if it means I'm not as prepared for a class or a meeting, so be it. The sermon has the greatest potential for individual and corporate life change, so it is the priority of my week. The pulpit is powerful, and sermon preparation is the best use of my time each week.

Tapping into the Power Source

Have you ever preached a weak sermon? I have—lots of them. Sermons that seem to go over the heads of the audience, sermons that were so simple the hearers learned nothing new, sermons without good news, sermons without a specific application, sermons without biblical authority—if there is a way to preach a powerless sermon I've probably done it. Let me suggest three ways to infuse your sermons with power.

A Good Foundation

The first and most obvious way is to *preach the Word*. Paul wrote to the Romans, "I am not ashamed of the gospel, because it is the power of God for the salvation of everyone who believes: first for the Jew, then for the Gentile" (Romans 1:16).

When I speak of preaching the Word, I am referring to a sermon that is drawn from an understanding of a biblical text—an "expository" or "exegetical" sermon. The sermon should attempt to communicate the main point of the biblical text on which it is based. When asked by a student how many points the ideal sermon should have, the teacher quipped, "At least one." A sermon can have any number of things at its beginning. It can have a joke, a striking statement, the results of a survey, and so on. It can end with a summary, a story, a poem, or something similar. But it can have only one thing at its core. It must have a biblical text. A sermon without a text is like a sailboat without a rudder. The wind can billow through the sails, the ship can look majestic, but it's probably heading for the rocks. To have powerful preaching, the sermon must be based on responsible study and exposition of the Bible.

When I begin sermon preparation, I start with a biblical text. I read it, reflect on it, study in the original language if possible, and attempt to draw out the main point. Only after this will I look at a commentary as an aid to understanding the text. After this I might read a sermon on the text by someone else. If I start here, I often short-circuit the process of understanding the text for myself. Finally, I will search for stories and illustrations to fill out the sermon. The Scripture itself must be at the core of the sermon. It is the foundation on which the whole sermon is built.

To infuse our sermons with power, it is essential that we plug into the power source. As the writer of Hebrews reminds us, "For the word of God is living and active. Sharper than any double-edged sword, it penetrates even to dividing soul and spirit, joints and marrow; it judges the thoughts and attitudes of the heart" (Hebrews 4:12). If a surgeon needs to cut me open and fix something, I want him to use a sharp scalpel. In the same way, if our congregation needs spiritual surgery, only the Word of God has the power to cut and to heal.

Creativity

A second way to tap into the power source is to use the creative power of your mind. Preachers know that a "Saturday Night Special" is not a cheap handgun or a meat loaf at the diner. It's a sermon, usually not very original or convicting, that goes from zero to complete in a couple of hours on Saturday evening (or Sunday morning, if you have the gift of procrastination). Saturday night specials are like microwave dinners. They have their occasional place, but a steady diet of them will stunt your congregation's growth.

Sermon preparation should be more like cooking in a crock-pot than a microwave oven. I love it when we cook food in the crock-pot. You gather the ingredients, put them in the pot, and let them simmer all day. Don't you love coming home to the fragrance of a crock-pot meal?

What is a crock-pot sermon? It's a sermon that develops over time. Sometimes this means working on a sermon a little every day. I recently listened to a sermon series by a well-known preacher. I was impressed with the content of the sermon and especially his illustrations. I wrote him a note and asked him to share with me his system for capturing and cataloging so many excellent illustrations. He wrote me back and almost apologetically indicated that he had no system—no files, no computer program. All he did was know what he was going to preach a year in advance, and as he would read something that applied he would copy it into a file. No, he did not have a "system" in a conventional sense. He had something better. He planned out his work and used the power of his mind to his advantage.

Do you ever find the perfect illustration or story the Monday after preaching a sermon on that topic? It happens to me a lot. It probably always will. But if you plan your work in advance, you can uncover some great material ahead of time.

So here's the approach I've adopted. My sermon preparation process for a calendar year begins in the late fall of the previous year. First, I lay out the kinds of sermon series I plan to preach for the coming year. Our elders develop a theme for the year, so some sermons will support it. I usually introduce the theme in January and come back to it periodically through the year. Early in the year I like to start a sermon series through a portion of the gospels. This is usually my longest series and will run through Easter.

After Easter I usually develop a topical series related to our theme. I treat Mother's Day and Father's Day as special days and work to fit sermon series around them.

During the summer it is difficult to preach sermons that build on each other since many of our members travel. In the summer I usually plan a couple of short topical series.

I find that the fall, when everyone is back from vacation, is a good time to start a new sermon series. I will often preach through an epistle or develop a series on a major theme of the Bible. This series will go to Thanksgiving, after which I usually prepare a short series leading up to Christmas.

It seems to me that my congregation prefers shorter sermon series. I try to preach series consisting of four to eight week segments. Most of the older planned preaching resources tended to encourage a quarterly sermon series. Shorter series keep the material fresh for me and for my congregation.

To assist with the process of gathering resources, I prepare a folder for each sermon series. As I run across material that might be helpful, I put a note in the folder briefly describing the material and where to find it. As a series approaches, I will prepare a folder for each individual sermon and place notes and material in the folder. Since I am working ahead, there is rarely a last-minute scramble for a commentary or article.

In a typical week I will work on four sermons. First, I begin study of the sermon I will preach in four weeks. This involves studying the passage and trying to determine the main idea that will form the sermon. Second, I continue study of the sermon I will preach in three weeks. I read commentaries to test my understanding of the passage and develop an outline. Third, I fill in the outline of the sermon I will preach in two weeks by adding illustrations I've accumulated along the way. And finally I put the finishing touches on the sermon I will preach the coming Sunday.

I typically schedule 8-10 hours of sermon preparation per week, usually two hour blocks of uninterrupted time during four weekdays and a couple of hours over the weekend to look over my Sunday sermon. I'm convinced that working ahead improves the quality of a sermon. It gives my mind an opportunity to meditate on the sermon, and I have an extended period of time to gather resources.

Another great reason to work ahead is that I never know what a week will bring. I can talk about a typical week, but we know there is no such thing. I can schedule some things. Usually weddings are placed on the calendar well in advance, but no one has ever made an appointment to talk about his funeral next Thursday! Sunday and Wednesday classes come every week, but I never know when I will have a call to the hospital. If I have an unusually heavy week of appointments, I do what needs to be done knowing I only need a couple of hours to finish this week's sermon. To me this is the best reason for working ahead. Even if I have two funerals, a wedding, several members in the hospital, and numerous exceptional situations to take care of, I can get my sermon finished in a couple of hours and be prepared for Sunday. Inevitably the crisis will pass, and I can catch up by scheduling a little extra sermon preparation time over the next couple of weeks.

Working ahead can be a struggle. It is difficult to maintain self-discipline. It is easy to let other things crowd out advance preparation. We already have busy schedules. But the best advice I can give to preachers who want to preach with power is to work ahead. Working ahead improves sermon quality and can have the effect of smoothing out the busy-ness in our schedules.

Innovation

A third way to infuse your sermons with power is to try new things. Have you noticed that we serve a creative God? I live in the northeastern United States, and my favorite time of the year is mid-October to early November. All summer the trees are a uniform olive green. As summer yields to autumn, the trees burst forth in innumerable shades of yellow, orange, and red. God is a creative God, and he created us to be creative. But often our sermons follow a predictable pattern. Our listeners can be lulled to a comatose state by a repetitive pattern of introduction, three points, and conclusion. Why not shake things up a little by trying new things?

One way to do this is by saving a little suspense for the end. Most sermons are deductive—the preacher states his main point up front and develops his sermon to prove the point. This is a time-honored and comfortable way to structure a sermon. What if you developed your sermon to lead to a main point at the end? Nathan's talk with King David in 2 Samuel 12 is a great example of this. Nathan did not say, "Today I would like to state three reasons why Jewish kings should hold themselves to high standards of moral conduct." Instead he told a story about two men, one wealthy and one poor. When the wealthy man took the poor man's lamb rather than one of his own, the Bible says, "David burned with anger against the man." Once Nathan got the emotional response from David, he was ready to lower the boom: "You are the man!" (2 Samuel 12:5, 7).

Can you imagine getting this kind of emotional involvement in a sermon? One way to keep your listeners engaged, even on the edge of their chairs, is to use the inductive model. Lead your listeners along with you and help them discover the main point for themselves.

Another way to be creative is to use props or visuals to help people "see" the point. Some people remember things they hear. Others are more visual—you have to show them and they will understand. I believe that if people can hear something, write it down (I include a simple outline in the worship bulletin) and see it, I've given them a reasonably good opportunity to understand the Word of God.

One way to do this is through the use of PowerPoint® slides. I try to do more than include my outline on the slides. I try to include pictures so that hopefully the main idea will be remembered.

Video clips are another visual way to teach. If you have the skill or if someone in your congregation does, you can produce your own video clips. Our campus minister wanted to give the congregation a sense of spirituality on the campus of the University of Delaware. He grabbed his video camera, went out to the main gathering place on campus, and started asking questions. When he showed the video in church, the congregation had a good understanding of the work that needed to be done on campus. Even if you don't have the talent to make your own, there are plenty of good resources out there to visually illustrate the truth you are trying to communicate.

I've also used props. A few years ago we scheduled a "neighbor day" for the middle of September. It happened to be the same weekend as the Jewish holy day Yom Kippur, the Day of Atonement. With a little checking around, we found that the granddaughter of one of our members owned a pet goat. We made costumes out of sheets and had one of our teens outfitted as the high priest. We brought the goat in and showed the congregation how the "scapegoat" was sent out. But we did not stop there. While the Day of Atonement and sending out of the scapegoat were repeated every year, the cross was a once for all event. To symbolize the permanence of forgiveness of sins at the cross, we invited each member of the congregation to write a sin they were struggling with on a card and bring it forward to a cross we set up at the front of our auditorium. At the foot of the cross was a shredder. Each person placed his or her card in the shredder, and it was gone forever. People still remember the day we had a goat in our assembly! They heard the story, they saw it enacted, they saw it fulfilled in Jesus, and they experienced the fullness of our forgiveness in him. And it stuck with them.

The Bible contains records of many preachers who used props to illustrate a message from God. A partial list might include a large boat (Noah), a staff (Moses), the scapegoat (the high priest), twelve stones (Joshua), children (Jesus), and belts (Agabus).

Lately we've seen a resurgence of interest in the "first-person" sermon. In my experience, a first-person sermon is one of the most creative, stressful, and rewarding preaching experiences. Through first-person sermons our congregation has had the opportunity to "meet" Bible characters and hear their side of the story. One of the more challenging stories in the New Testament is the Parable of the Unjust Steward (Luke 16). To help the congregation understand the story, we had a newspaper reporter interview the steward's coworker. One holiday season Herod the Great and Joseph, the earthly father of Jesus, paid us a visit.

First-person sermons give preachers and congregations an opportunity to see the biblical story through a different set of characters. Sometimes getting another perspective helps us understand the story better for ourselves.

I find first-person preaching stressful. The sermon usually requires more research. And of course it must be memorized—it wouldn't be very realistic to have a character get up and read his story. To top it off, creativity is not one of my spiritual gifts! Thankfully, others are creative. Numerous books and audio resources are available to teach you how to present a first-person sermon. Maybe there are creative people in your congregation who can help you. Perhaps there is a talented person who would do a first-person sermon if someone helped write it. Trying a new approach can be a challenge, but I remember how I felt after each sermon where I took this kind of risk. I felt drained yet fulfilled, knowing I had helped the congregation see the story in a new way.

Another way to improve creativity is to involve others in the planning and preparation of sermons. A few years ago we identified "inspiring worship" as an area of church life we needed to improve. Out of this realization came an "assembly planning team" to improve both technical and creative aspects of our assemblies. We meet monthly, and one of the agenda items is future sermon topics. At one of the meetings I shared that I was preaching a sermon on Tabitha as an example of ministry to the poor. A week or so later a video clip showed up from one of the team members. It was a video from our Vacation Bible School that showed one of the characters "shooing off" the beggars walking around the village. At first I did not see how the video clip could fit into the sermon. But I thought about it, talked with others about it, and through the discussion realized that the clip illustrated one possible response to the poor. So the sermon evolved from "Christians should help the poor" to "There is a range of responses to helping the poor—what are you going to do?" The collaboration made the sermon practical and effective.

In an age when we are bombarded with sound bites and visual images, it is valuable—if not imperative—to use creativity in preaching. Creativity in sermon structure, visual aids, an occasional first-person sermon, and drawing on the talents of others can give our congregations new ways to hear and experience the life-changing gospel.

Powerful Biblical Teaching

In most churches, Bible classes form an integral part of Christian education. Many smaller churches rely on their preacher as the main adult class teacher. I've already explained my priority with respect to preaching and other responsibilities. Some of the points I made regarding preaching apply to Bible class preparation. Planning and working ahead is imperative given the often-chaotic schedules we keep. Creativity is a plus in any setting.

Bible class settings vary widely. There is often the "auditorium class" where the teacher stands in front and the participants sit facing him. Other classes meet in classrooms or fellowship rooms where a more informal setting is possible. I try to encourage smaller, more informal class settings because I believe the Bible class can accomplish different objectives than the sermon.

First, a Bible class is one place to get a good discussion going. Here the collective wisdom and knowledge of the members can be brought to bear on the Scriptures. I find that the best Bible class teachers are those who have mastered the art of asking good questions. Good questions are open-ended, requiring more than a yes or no answer. Good questions have variety. Some question content of the passage, others the motive, and others call the hearer to apply the text. While in a sermon I have to do all of the above, in a discussion-oriented Bible class the students can participate and enrich our understanding of the text.

Second, a Bible class is a good gauge of where your people are spiritually. Through give and take you can learn more about your people and how to help them grow in their relationship with God. Here's something I uncovered recently. Some people will talk all day about the text, but if you ask them to apply the truth to their lives, they fall silent. Others are happy to say what they think, but they never really engage the text. This kind of information helps me tailor the class to the spiritual maturity and needs of the members.

One final note about discussion-oriented Bible classes: they are a great source of stories, quips, and quotes. When I teach a Bible class, I keep a pen ready because I never know what kind of a gem I might uncover for later use!

Pass It On

A church cannot expand the number of Bible classes offered without qualified teachers to teach them. We wanted to develop new teachers, so our deacon of adult education put together a class we called Biblical Preaching and Teaching. One quarter every year we offer a beginning or advanced class to train teachers and supply preachers for our congregation.

It is not a typical Bible class—we require the students to do outside reading (*Biblical Preaching* by Haddon Robinson is our preferred text) and come prepared to discuss the material. By the end we expect them to prepare an outline for a class or sermon and briefly present it to the class.

Those who complete the assignments are given a Sunday to preach or teach the material they prepared. Once they present the material to the church, the class gives the speaker feedback. Through this process we have discovered new sources of preaching and teaching talent, and we have equipped those who desire to preach or teach with the tools to do an effective job. Most importantly, we have fulfilled the role of leaders stated in Ephesians 4:12, "to prepare God's people for works of service, so that the Body of Christ may be built up until we all reach unity in the faith and in the knowledge of the Son of God and become mature, attaining to the whole measure of the fullness of Christ."

Years ago I ventured to the pulpit, largely unprepared, for the first time. A lot of what I've learned over the years has been through trial and error. You can accelerate the growth process for a young man in your congregation by intentionally working with him to develop his preaching and teaching talent. Few things are as rewarding as seeing someone you train go on to have an effective ministry, whether in the pulpit or classroom. Are you up for the challenge?

Pulling It All Together

The greatest power source for the small congregation—and in fact for any congregation of God's people—is the Word of God. Time invested in planning, study, and creativity will reap a bountiful harvest in your congregation. I've shared some things that work for me. Make sure your sermons and classes are built on the foundation of God's Word, the true power source. Plan ahead and work ahead to unleash the power of your mind. Use creative, memorable methods to present the sermon. And take the things you've learned and intentionally pass them on to others.

Paul reminded Timothy, "The elders who direct the affairs of the church well are worthy of double honor, especially those whose work is preaching and teaching" (1 Timothy 5:17). If your work involves preaching and teaching, you are to be honored by the congregation. I hope they recognize and appreciate your work. And I hope you will approach your task with renewed zeal, knowing the Lord desires to change lives through your preaching and teaching.

CHAPTER FOUR

LIFE AT HOME:
PRESERVING AND PROTECTING
THE LEADER'S FAMILY LIFE

BARRY P. KLEIN

CHRISTIAN MARRIAGES AND CHRISTIAN FAMILIES are fantastic, challenging, mysterious, and wonderful! No wonder the apostle Paul in 1 Corinthians 7:7 refers to marriage as a gift (as he also does with singleness). Because there is so much to explore and discover in a church leader's marriage and family, let me share a little about my own marriage and family.

We are a family of five. My wife and I have been married since 1979, and we have three grown children (one daughter and two sons). We are entering a new phase in our family. As I write we are anticipating our daughter's wedding, our older son's college graduation, and our younger son's high school graduation. We have been ministering with the Church of Christ in Staples, Minnesota, since 1999.

Incorporated in 1889 and first named Presto, the community of Staples has a population of 3,100 people and covers portions of two counties. The two counties together combine for a population of 38,282 people. Staples is a town with a rich railroad heritage. Both freight and Amtrak trains frequently come through town. We are part of a consolidated school district. We have a growing health care system with a new hospital. A 3M plant is also here among dozens of other businesses. A delightful growing community of Amish are among us. We are about 125 miles northwest of Minneapolis–St. Paul.

The Church of Christ in Staples, Minnesota, incorporated in 1913. We are a congregation of about 140 people. We have three elders, a volunteer secretary, and ministry teams that include worship, missions, fellowship, and quilting. We have small groups for men and women. We are searching for a second staff person and are experimenting with a second service.

Finding Family Roots

The idea of family is deeply significant to my wife and me—both biblically and experientially. As we serve the church, we see a wonderful and challenging interplay between biological and spiritual family. God describes himself in Scripture as our Father (Psalm 68:5; 89:26: Isaiah 9:6; Matthew 6:4, 9; 2 Corinthians 1:2), and we find family securely placed in the midst of our own stories. As the traditional family finds itself under attack in our culture, Psalm 68:5 offers solace and hope, reminding us that God is "a father to the fatherless, a defender of widows."

Ministering to people with deep emotional and spiritual needs requires that we come alongside them with God's love, hope, and direction. We need to come not as accusers, but as co-travelers. We need to strike a balance between principle and process. This includes remembering that in the midst of sharing God's living truths, the way in which those truths are shared and applied must be gentle and tailored to the individual or couple. Even Christian leaders' families are characterized by a variety of relational styles. William J. Petersen's book, *25 Surprising Marriages: Faith-Building Stories from the Lives of Famous Christians* (Baker Books, 1997) describes this reality. When our hearts are right before the Lord, we will be sensitive to style, timing, and patience as we help the families in our churches apply God's truth to their lives.

We live in a cultural smorgasbord of human ideas. As a result we must be skilled, sensitive, and humble as we come alongside hurting people who are disengaged from the family of God, the family of civic community, their family of origin, or their immediate family. We come as player-coaches. As coaches, we help, listen, and guide. As players, we come with an awareness of our own imperfections and how far we have yet to go in our own journey.

An Oxymoron

In Mark 7:9-13 Jesus spoke with the Pharisees and teachers of the law about their religious traditions. He challenged them to rethink their preoccupation with external obedience to law and ceremony to the neglect of their inner world. Quoting from Isaiah 29:13 Jesus admonished them to recognize that their hearts were far from God. He continued to challenge their view of religious leadership, a view that disconnected ministry to family from ministry to God. The heart of the discussion can be found in verses 11-13 when Jesus, quoting them, says, "But you say that if a man says to his father or mother: 'Whatever help you might otherwise have received from me is Corban' (that is, a gift devoted to God), then you no longer let him do anything for his father or mother. Thus you nullify the word of God by your tradition that you have handed down. And you do many things like that." God wants us to serve him by serving our families.

God isn't pleased when he is pitted against marriage and the family. He created the family. He ordained marriage. We only add to the injustice when we try to justify our neglect of family on religious grounds. Charity still begins at home!

God's name and honor are at stake in the way we serve and nurture our families. Men often struggle with the temptation to provide financially, even willingly working longer hours, to avoid engaging in the dynamics of home life. But it isn't only a male temptation. One of our local female physicians once remarked how much easier it was to practice medicine than to be at home with her young child!

It is true that we are to love God more than family, as Jesus clearly teaches in Matthew 10:37. But Jesus' example is one of incarnational love to us. He didn't pit his love for his Father against us. He often loved his Father by loving us (see Romans 8:31, 32).

Paul commended the Macedonian Christians who had shared their financial resources so freely and said of them, "And they did not do as we expected, but they gave themselves first to the Lord and then to us in keeping with God's will" (2 Corinthians 8:5). What an encouraging reminder to church leaders who live as models to others. We need to be personally present, giving ourselves, our time, and our hearts to our mates, children, and extended family. Money has its place, but giving to our families by listening, helping, empathizing, and guiding are far greater gifts.

My wife maintains our family schedule and has reminded me through the years to include my ministry obligations and appointments on our family calendar. We make sure my ministry calendar and our family calendar "talk to each other." Our children's events are no less important than church appointments. They need us to be present at their events, spurring them on, congratulating them, helping them bear their mistakes and losses. So many films like *I Am Sam, The Christmas Box, The Bishop's Wife,* and *The Story Lady* bring out the rippling cost of neglecting home life. No one on his deathbed wishes he had spent more time at the office.

The Households of Family and Church

How are you investing yourself in the lives of your mate and your children, especially if those children are still at home? Have you ever asked the members of your family how they feel about your investment in their lives? Church leaders need to consider the impact of their family life on the life of the church. The apostle Paul spoke to this in 1 Timothy 3:4, 5 when he wrote that an elder "must manage his own family well and see that his children obey him with proper respect. (If anyone does not know how to manage his own family, how can he take care of God's church?)."

Before we discuss the meaning of the word *manage*, let's focus on a related dynamic. Often church leaders are called to a higher standard in marriage and family life. With this higher standard comes a calling and equipping by God. We need to be clear about the source of this calling and the provision that accompanies the calling. Put another way, we cannot afford midstream to accuse God of being unfair by expecting more from us in our marriages and families because we are church leaders. I have often told my wife that if push comes to shove between our marriage and the ministry, our marriage will be the one to survive the battle. That has given her assurance and comfort to remain beside me in the challenges of the ministry.

So what does "manage his own family" mean? Several translations use the word *rule. The Cotton Patch Version* says, "should do a good job running." The word picture is of one "rightly standing in front of" his family. Christians in authority serve others. God himself provides the example and calls us to be benevolent leaders as we serve our mates, children, and others. If we manage our families by force or demand, we have lost the heart of Jesus' command in Luke 22:24-27. When we consider biblical descriptions of God and his leaders, we see shepherds who exercise compassion, courage, skill, patience, and wisdom. Ezekiel 34 reminds us of how the leaders of God's people had forgotten (or never discovered) what it means to live in the example of God as the shepherd. We need regularly to ask, "Am I managing, am I being in front of" my wife and children as a Psalm 23 and John 10 shepherd? These relationships are the fertile ground from which springs that pastoral, protective, and leading love a church leader shows to the local church family. Think of it this way: the character of Jesus, as the Good Shepherd, draws us to him. This is a distant cry from forced leadership. Sheep are not designed to be driven. People are designed to be led by truth in love (Ephesians 4:15).

Keeping the Home Fires Burning

A family man who is also a church leader needs to live with a keen sense of kingdom priorities. But this can be (and often is) countercultural in our fast-paced, materialistic, get-ahead world. In his book *Margin* (NavPress, 1992), Dr. Richard Swenson reminds us that "We must have some room to breathe. We need freedom to think and permission to heal. Our relationships are being starved to death by velocity. No one has the time to listen, let alone love. Our children lay wounded on the ground, run over by our high-speed good intentions. Is God now pro-exhaustion? Doesn't he lead people by the still waters any more?" Apparently every generation needs to learn this, for a similar warning was echoed over a century ago by Charles Wagner in his book, *The Simple Life* (J.S. Ogilvie Publishing Company, 1904).

Earlier I mentioned the importance of soliciting feedback from your spouse and children about the quality of relationships you share with them. We dare not assume our perception is accurate, let alone healthy. Take the initiative to ask questions like "Is there anything you need from me that you are not receiving?" or "Is there any unfinished business between us?" Be ready for awkward moments. Pray in advance that your heart and theirs will be soft and receptive. The more this kind of invitation becomes a way of life, the less awkward it will be.

In 1 Timothy 5:8 Paul wrote, "If anyone does not provide for his relatives, and especially for his immediate family, he has denied the faith and is worse than an unbeliever." If we have ever wondered how far Jesus' words in Mark 7:9-13 apply to our care and responsibility for our immediate family, we should wonder no more. First Timothy 3:4, 5 and 1 Timothy 5:8 indicate that God is talking about the family under our roof!

I have been profoundly affected by the life of Marilee Pierce Dunker as reflected in her book *Man of Vision, Woman of Prayer* (Thomas Nelson Publisher, 1980). Marilee is the daughter of the late Bob Pierce, founder of World Vision, International. She writes about the great things her father did for God, but at the devastating price of his marriage and family. It is an agonizing book to read (and at the same time I would consider it must reading for any church leader who feels tempted to sacrifice marriage and family on the altar of ministry). The book had another title originally: Days of Glory, Seasons of Night. The former referred to her father; the latter to her mother. Havoc and dysfunction reigned in their house during his lengthy absences and his infrequent times at home.

At times we may feel the responsibility of caring for our immediate family is simply too great. Admitting this can be a starting place to reflect, evaluate, and change. A sacrificial spirit grows out of putting on Christ and his character. The deeper our love for God and our families, the less we will be conscious of any sacrifice. It is both a privilege and responsibility to be entrusted with a mate and children. We need to consider what Jesus left in Heaven (Philippians 2) in order to fulfill his Father's costly plan of paying the price for our sins. Then we will more clearly see how small our "sacrifice" is in comparison to his.

Many couples today bring increasingly complex problems and perceptions into their marriages. The local church must rise to this challenge and give them a model of healthy marriages that grow in intimacy while putting God first. This also allows the local church to prepare couples for marriage (even before premarital counseling) in a way that will better equip them to lead and serve the church.

From Theory to Practice

When it comes to protecting and preserving life at home, ministry leaders and volunteers must be prepared to move from theory to practice. At some point they must be willing to enter the proverbial "tunnel of chaos" and take a difficult inventory of their family relationships. Ask members of your family and others who know you well to give you an honest assessment of the kind of husband and father you are to your family. Making this a regular (at least yearly) process is vital for making mid-course adjustments. Take the initiative. Welcome the pruning, refining, and even the rebukes if they are to God's glory.

Taking Action in Our Marriages

- Once Cindy and I became engaged, I began asking God to provide and sustain a "divine excitement" or spark throughout our marriage. Although selfishness seems always to lurk around the corner, God has been faithful to answer that prayer. I thank him often for his gift.
- I regularly put Cindy's name (including endearing nicknames) in songs, singing to her and about her.
- I pay close attention to her intuition about safe and unsafe women. (It took me a while to learn the value of this.)
- I write encouraging entries in a notebook that recount memories and events we have shared along with words of appreciation. Cindy has complete access to the notebook. I anticipate it's greater value for her if I precede her in death.
- Before we go to sleep, I put my arm around her and pray, thanking God for giving me such a special wife and friend.
- We talk matters through before making decisions.
- I keep a notebook containing reflections on our marriage that I share with Cindy.
- Years ago, I wrote an essay I called "Tribute to the Delight of My Eyes." I included copies of the essay in our children's journals also. I also wrote a poem that hangs on our bedroom wall describing key life-chapter details from our courtship to the present.

- I regularly ask the Lord to help me love Cindy as Christ loved the church.
- I keep in mind that the church already has a husband.

Taking Action in Our Parenting

Recently I asked my 21-year-old son to give me a list of things he remembered and appreciated about our family life as he was growing up. Here's what he had to say.

- Walking us to school.
- Resting in bed and talking with us.
- Never yelling.
- Confronting in private.
- Giving honest answers to our personal questions and struggles.
- Being available for quality time.
- Limiting TV time to the time our family spent together watching programs.
- Distinguishing between personal and moral issues (ear piercing, for example).
- Being open to questions about life.
- Asking what I needed from him at varying steps of life.
- Writing to us in his journal
- Holding up Christ, our mother, and us as priorities.
- Admitting mistakes and seeking forgiveness.
- Making his quiet time with God a priority while being available to us.
- Accepting my apologies for interrupting or bothering by saying, "No, you're never a bother."
- Encouraging us through cards, e-mails, and phone calls.
- Supporting and loving us no matter what.
- Showing respect and faithfulness to Mom.
- Displaying kindness and seeking reconciliation when wronged.

I asked our 24-year-old daughter to provide a similar list.

- Scheduling intentional dates with me for breakfast.
- Taking time to talk about things we were dealing with (life, relationships, and so on). This has become more valuable to me as I've grown older.
- Stopping what he was doing if we needed him, even when he was working against a deadline.
- Watching my dad love my mom; I found out from my friends that my parents' relationship wasn't necessarily typical in other families.
- Receiving letters and cards weekly from Dad while I was in college. This made me feel loved and remembered.
- Putting up the Christmas tree together, decorating the outside of the house, driving around looking at Christmas lights, and going Christmas caroling with the church family.
- Making family visits a priority no matter how far we had to drive. Nearly all our family vacations included visits to our family on the east or west coast.
- Teaching us that time with people and relationships are more valuable than things.

If I Were Starting Over

- I would listen to Cindy earlier about "being above reproach" in my interactions with women in ministry. Specifically, I would have followed her advice from the beginning never to meet privately with another woman.
- I would be more protective of my wife in ministry. Cindy and I have worked closely together in ministry throughout our marriage. The down side of this is that some have had unfair expectations of her role in the church family.
- I would be less of a perfectionist.
- I would be quicker to identify and avoid the things that waste time and resources.
- I would be less judgmental.

Parting Thoughts

From time to time my wife will tell me, "Pencil us into your calendar." Most of us end up doing what is on our calendars. Include time with your spouse and children when you plan your hours, days, weeks, and months.

Here's a definition of marriage I often share with couples: "Marriage is a union before God of a man and woman on a lifetime journey as husband and wife, where each person goes only as far as both can go together in Christ." As schedules permit, my wife rides her bike with me while I run. We travel most of the route together, side by side, on the rural roads of Staples. At times we separate on the journey, but we begin and end together. It works this way because we plan ahead, travel in the same direction, and communicate together. Intentional, planned communication is essential.

Church leaders must build accountability into their lives. I keep a time sheet that tracks personal and pastoral time increments every 15 minutes of my day. I voluntarily submit this tool to my elders with the understanding that they can ask any question of me.

Create a buffer zone for your family. Life's bumps and bruises, especially for children, are increasing at an alarming rate. For our own families as well as for teaching the church by example, we need to help cushion the cruelty the world pours on our children. We can do this by being available, being good listeners, and helping our children in the process of dealing with and learning from life's mistakes.

At our elders' meetings, we often pray for each other's marriages and families.

Remember to pray daily for your wife and children. Ask God to help you love your wife as Christ loved the church and to love your children with a love that points them to their Father in Heaven.

CHAPTER FIVE

ELDERS <small>AND</small> OTHER LEADERS:
BUILDING POSITIVE RELATIONSHIPS
<small>FOR</small> EFFECTIVE DECISION MAKING

BRIAN INGALLS

I T'S GOING TO BE TEMPTING, throughout this chapter, for you to say to yourself, "We could never do that at our church. The men here would never go for something like this." You might be right. Remember, however, that God didn't call you to be a leader of his church so you could base your long-term vision on your ability. He called you to rely on his ability. He is the same God who parted the Red Sea, the same God who took twelve untrained, unschooled men and turned them into apostles who led the early church. While you certainly will face difficult and uncertain days ahead, I am convinced God can change hearts and give a vision to the oldest, the most stubborn, or the most hard-headed among us. Paul would be exhibit A if you need a biblical reference. If you'd like a modern day, smaller church exhibit, I'd offer up Plains Christian Church in Plains, Kansas.

A Near-Death Experience

Before God called me into the ministry and long before I became the minister at Plains, my wife and I joined Plains Christian Church as a newlywed couple, freshly moved to Kansas, where I was starting a career in agribusiness. I've seen the before and after of PCC. When we joined as members, the signs of a slow church death were all around us: low attendance, lack of participation, very little in the way of programming, and a lack of money so severe it took three board meetings to approve filling the cracks in the concrete porch at the front door. The problems were particularly sad considering the nice people who attended.

For quite some time the church had no other meetings besides Sunday morning—a fact that led my wife and me to participate on Sunday nights and Wednesdays with another church twenty miles away. Eventually, through the other church, God led us into the ministry. In the meantime, however, the ministers hired at Plains Christian Church typically preached well, worked hard at a VBS and camp, and held revivals from time to time, but nothing seemed to work. The church, despite the efforts and wishes of the leaders and members, was growing older and smaller.

In some ways, the near-death experience of Plains Christian Church was an advantage. In a pivotal board meeting which happened long after I had entered the ministry and moved away, the board of Plains Christian Church (all 2 or 3 of them) decided they would hire one more minister instead of closing the doors. They no longer had the money to pay someone full-time wages, but with a final step of faith, they trusted God. Facing such stark reality, the members were ready for change. Ready for anything, in fact! Without something different, the doors would close, and they knew it. So they hired a guy from Texas. Now that's faith born out of desperation, isn't it? A Texan!

Wait, I was born in Dallas . . .

A New Day

His name was Jim Dunn. Jim was just plain different from anything this church had seen in a long time. He had the audacity to believe God had bigger plans for our small congregation than simply to fade away into history. Not only did Jim believe God was going to do more with our church, he worked diligently through teaching and preaching to convince the members of this. In church lingo these days, we like to refer to this as "communicating a vision."

I dislike that phase. It sounds like a business idea, but this isn't new, and it isn't just for corporations. "Communicating a vision" is biblical. Jim was following the example of Christ when he labored to help other people see what he could see. Jim helped build other's faith in God, just as Jesus had encouraged, prodded, taught, modeled, and helped his disciples learn to have faith so many years ago. In Jim's case, this meant helping the entire church of 15 people understand that God could and would do great things at Plains Christian Church. Here was a guy who didn't just say God could grow the church; he was expecting it.

Think about how crazy this must have seemed. Plains, Kansas, is a community of farmers, agribusiness, oil companies, schools, and small hospitals. Thirty percent or more of the 1,163 residents are Hispanic. Seven miles away, the nearby town of Kismet, Kansas has a whopping population of 500 with the same makeup, and Meade, Kansas, is 15 miles away with 1,600 mostly Caucasian residents. Often people here move to bigger cities and better jobs. In fact, when my wife and I first arrived, our goal wasn't to put down roots, but eventually to move on to bigger and better things in our careers. I remarked to my wife while standing outside in the city of Plains, surrounded by flat, Kansas land stretching for miles with only a few trees dotting the landscape, that this is what it must be like to use a gymnasium as your bedroom. There was way too much space!

Jim must have thought he was looking at five loaves and two fish and figured with God, a little goes a long way. His wife Meredith formed a children's ministry team, and the church began to formulate a vision for children's and youth ministries. As Jim preached, the congregation grew from 15 to 60 to 100 and suddenly a new sanctuary was built. Plains Christian Church was actually growing! The church reached 200 before Jim left. In Houston, Texas, this wouldn't register, but here 200 represents more than ten percent of our little town. Since I replaced Jim as the senior minister during the last two and a half years, we have continued to run 200, despite the fact that during this time sixteen families from our church have moved away from our community to take new jobs.

Today, we have contemporary services, a weekly talk-radio program, a large children's ministry and facility, a downtown youth center (minus a real downtown) where our youth groups are headquartered, and an associate minister. We have hosted a Small Town Church Conference, large evangelistic events, and sent tens of thousands of dollars every year to mission work. Our youth and adults regularly travel on mission trips, to conferences, and to other events. This year, over a hundred people will accept Christ as their Savior because of the ministry of Plains Christian Church. Our church leadership gets things done like no other group of men I've ever been around. While many churches our size struggle to fund the smallest projects or start new ministries, we struggle to keep from doing too much. It's an amazing story, but don't think for a minute it's easy.

Plains Christian Church is a mixture of highly organized people and highly disorganized people. We have nurses, school teachers, coaches, managers, union employees, farmers, agribusiness workers, the self-employed, the rarely employed, retirees, military personnel, and more. A church filled with young parents, we face all the issues and dangers associated with divorce, alcoholism, parenting, gossip, and struggles of every kind. Since our church is continually growing, the backgrounds of our people vary from Catholic to Protestant and everything in between—all crammed currently into only 200 people on Sunday morning.

Oh yeah, and we have a relatively inexperienced minister. How's that for obstacles? Praise God, he can overcome anything! So understanding that we are still learning and that God is not finished with us, I hope to offer some insights into what we've learned about elders, deacons, and church boards as we've grown this far and as God prepares us to take the next steps in ministry.

Our Need

When I was in college studying for a degree in business, JIT was the rage. It stands for Just In Time—an inventory system manufacturers used to streamline their production by reducing the inventories of parts and materials to the bare minimum. Everything used in the production process had to be ordered constantly or produced constantly in order to keep the plant running. When one part or piece of material was finished at one stage, it would be sent to the next stage in the process "Just In Time" to be used. As you can imagine, if anything went wrong, the whole place could shut down.

What smaller inventories do for business, smaller numbers of members and smaller numbers in the community do for churches. They expose shortfalls and weaknesses in church ministry. People here notice when someone leaves, and it often hurts. Targeting a certain profile of people like Saddleback Church does is easier when there are 500,000 of them in your community. Smaller churches have to reach a broader spectrum of people simply because there aren't as many people. Besides, didn't Jesus call us to preach the gospel to every sort of person? Unfortunately, to do so requires flexibility, constant reevaluation, and change—not the easiest things to find in a church board meeting. Plus, the diversity of the community and the diversity of ages in any small town often present us with more needs than we have resources to meet. At least at first glance. How many times have we heard questions like: "Do you have a children's program on Wednesday night?" "Do you have anything for young adults?" (Here's a secret: If you have a children's program, you'll attract young adults.) The demand on church leaders and ministers to lead a small diverse group of people into unity and harmony is difficult, to say the least. For one thing, church members aren't always on the same page.

I have always had a heart for reaching people with the gospel, and I've found that most ministers and serious church members have the same heart. It's frustrating to me when the leaders of the church don't share this sense of urgency for the lost in their community. It doesn't take a focus group or research grant to figure out that many people who serve as elders and deacons have different ideas about why the church exists. There always seems to be a group of people who believe the body of Christ is here to conduct weddings, funerals, visit the sick, hold fellowship dinners and socials, and maintain a nice building in town for everyone to admire. Others, like you I hope, believe the church is God's missionary organization to your community to bring more and more people into the family of God. If this is you, congratulations! You've read your Bible!

But can you get those elders and deacons to desire the same thing? Will they ever see church ministry as a higher priority than a school function? Will they ever lead the church as men who understand the Great Commission? Can you get them to see the mission of the church the way you see it? At Plains Christian Church, the last question has been the key for us.

Meeting Our Need

In our church the elders, together with the minister, make decisions by consensus. We don't vote. We either agree or disagree, but things don't get done if we don't agree. There is no such thing, really, as a board meeting at Plains Christian. We have elders meetings and elders-deacons meetings. The elders make decisions and the deacons offer their input, serve officially as trustees on legal documents, and are there to help implement the ministries of the church. Since the minister conducts the meeting, he has a great opportunity to share his vision and bring up spiritual issues as well as business issues. Often someone will speak of a ministry that really worked a few years back or offer his opinion on what elements he'd like to see in a worship service. We're just as likely to gripe as we are to be gracious, but we rarely get through a meeting without laughing and visiting as if we had just finished dinner and the football game had gone to commercial.

The overall vision for the church, the direction of the church, and the steps needed to get there, are overseen by the minister with the elders' guidance. This arrangement is one of great influence and responsibility. And it's nothing new. Take a close look at the book of Titus. It's only three chapters long and can be skimmed pretty quickly. Go ahead, I'll wait . . .

. . . Now, what did you think?

Did you notice verses like this: "The reason I left you in Crete was that you might straighten out what was left unfinished and appoint elders in every town, as I directed you" (Titus 1:5)?

There is no mention here of calling a congregational meeting with a minimum of 60 days notice by letter indicating the time, place, and agenda for said meeting. It would be difficult to imagine Titus following *Robert's Rules of Order* for the meeting, and I doubt anyone took minutes. Titus had authority because he was a man of God, under God's authority and call. He chose men to be elders. There wasn't a vote. The decision was based on the leading of the Holy Spirit and certain guidelines and qualifications provided by Paul.

Or how about this verse? "You must teach what is in accord with sound doctrine. Teach the older men to be temperate, worthy of respect, self-controlled, and sound in faith, in love and in endurance. Likewise, teach the older women to be reverent in the way they live, not to be slanderers or addicted to much wine, but to teach what is good. . . . Similarly, encourage the young men to be self-controlled. In everything set them an example by doing what is good. In your teaching show integrity, seriousness and soundness of speech that cannot be condemned. . . . Encourage and rebuke with all authority. Do not let anyone despise you" (Titus 2:1-15, selected portions).

Paul expected Titus to be the leader, the director, the organizer, the example, and the person God used to mold not only the ministries of the church, but the behavior of the members of the congregation. I believe we are merely skimming the text if we do not recognize how many uncomfortable moments this must have presented to Titus as he carried out such orders.

For Timothy, it wasn't any different. "The elders who direct the affairs of the church well are worthy of double honor, especially those whose work is preaching and teaching" (1 Timothy 5:17).

If you whip out the ol' *King James Version* or look it up in the Greek, you'll find the word for "direct the affairs" literally means "rule" or "to be over." Paul would also command Timothy to rebuke others when necessary and to carry out such instructions without partiality.

This is a far different model of church leadership than we usually see in church boards or with the roles of elders and deacons of the church. I was certainly not accustomed to such responsibility being placed upon my shoulders. But I wasn't alone. Neither are you.

Getting There from Here

"I realized I had to decide if I wanted to be that man. Or if I even could."

Those words were spoken recently at a small church minister's conference by Willie Coop. As the minister of Westway Christian Church in Scottsbluff, Nebraska, a successful and growing church by most standards, Willie had noticed the churches that are succeeding today are churches with ministers who took charge—men of faith who were willing to stand up and tell the entire congregation, "Let's go this way!" These men listened intently to the Holy Spirit and communicated what God was laying on their heart, giving the members of the church a sense of purpose and direction. The greatest leaders in the Bible pushed, pulled, challenged, reminded, exhorted, and sometimes even gave orders. Then, like Paul, they developed more leaders to do the same thing. Ironically, while it is very common for ministers to spend hours preparing lessons and sermons, rarely do they spend much time preparing, praying, and studying for a board meeting or an elder's meeting. Rarely do they show up with a plan and a direction already in mind, planted there by the Holy Spirit.

At Plains Christian, the senior minister made disciples out of the men of our church by his example of faith—not just words from the pulpit. Taking the men on an outing or mission trip is helpful, but it is no substitute for the daily example of a leader who continually teaches, continually models the type of man he wants his elders and deacons to be, and who continually encourages the men to have faith in God. Obviously, one man cannot run every program and activity, but in many ways the minister is the man primarily responsible for watching over what goes on at the church and making sure something is going on! And the most amazing thing happened here: leadership brought unity. Facing conflict has led to accomplishing and reaching more. Doing away with the rules of order and unnecessary formality brought better cooperation, more honest input, more fellowship—and we get a lot more done.

Let's be honest. It might have been easier for Jim Dunn, and easier for me today, than it will be for you. Jim had a plan before he was hired to lead the church the way he believed God had laid out in the Bible, and Jim made his intentions clear at the start. Jim knew the type of leadership and church he wanted to mold Plains Christian Church into, but as it was for me and probably for many of you, this idea could be somewhat uncomfortable. I was used to a chairman of the board, to the minister sitting silently in the board meeting until it was time for him to give his "report," and for leadership training to revolve around a few conferences attended by less than half of the deacons and elders. I walked in and was immediately asked, "What do you want us to do? What's your vision?" Can you answer those questions about your congregation today?

I keep an old copy of our church bylaws. This particular set was amended and adopted in 1985. A yellow highlighter marks every page with handwritten notes in red ink-pen in the margins. It's Jim's handwriting. One particular note is just one word with a question mark: "Bible?" It's a good question because what is in the bylaws at that particular paragraph is not from the Bible, but from our traditions of church leadership. It's difficult for some churches to let go of traditions. It's difficult to change the way something has been done for 50 years, even if it has been done incorrectly all that time.

This is where we start—not with the bylaws necessarily, but with the Bible and with a heart submitted to the Bible. Jesus offended quite a few people when he drove the money changers out of the temple, but he did so based on Scripture. "It is written," he said to them, "'My house will be called a house of prayer,' but you are making it a 'den of robbers'" (Matthew 21:13). Jesus loved God's Word more than he loved the approval of men. So must we. The opportunity is already present in most of our churches. We already believe the Word. The common ground between ministers, elders, and deacons begins with the Bible. When it comes to the preaching and teaching of Scripture from the pulpit, to the board meeting, to the elders' meeting, every minister can make instruction in the Word of God part of what he says and the basis for any change he seeks to make.

I recently asked our men what they thought of the idea of appointing someone to be chairman of the board. An elder, one of the men who had been here from the early days, looked at me in the meeting and said, "Jim never wanted a chairman of the board. He said it wasn't biblical."

Not only was Jim right, he had taught these guys effectively. Everything begins with teaching the Word of God to the men and women you face in the meetings. That much seems obvious, but what seems to be missing often is the realization that most ministers already have a measure of spiritual authority and respect among most of the elders and deacons in their churches. Yet many only teach or preach in the classroom or from the pulpit. Should the preacher's passion only come out when he's on stage? I think many ministers would be surprised how easily the elders and deacons of their church would be open to a new vision if the minister were just as challenging and just as passionate in the board meeting. I was surprised. And why stop with board meetings? Ministers, when you were ordained, you were set apart for the gospel of Christ. It's not an occupation, it's who you are. Be that man.

A funny memory we have here is the day someone threw a copy of our bylaws at Jim. Literally. And part of using spiritual authority means addressing sin as well as holding the line against legalism. I was good at holding the line on legalism, but far too hesitant when it came to confronting sin. Yet both are necessary. However difficult it was, when we faced these issues with the Scripture as the basis of our authority, another amazing thing happened: everyone grew spiritually. Especially me! Often God allows conflicts and issues to crop up so you can grow too. It's like lifting weights. You must break the muscle down before it grows stronger. Jesus said the Father prunes the branches that bear fruit so they will bear even more. So hang in there.

That was number one. Start using the spiritual authority of your position and your calling. Instruct, teach, rebuke, and encourage. Do I sound like Paul yet? That's a big hint. This stuff is in the Bible.

Second, write it down. Whatever the vision, whatever the mission you feel God has for you, write it down. Discuss it with your leaders, talk about it in meetings and in regular conversations. Put it in the bulletin. Teach it in a Sunday school class or in a Bible study. New members at Plains Christian Church go through a class called PCC 101. We borrowed the idea and bought the materials from Saddleback, changing them to fit our needs. It is a great class for teaching new members what we believe, how we do things, and where we believe God is leading us. In your vision, in your ideas for the church, be specific. People don't latch on to vague visions; they do, however, latch on to building programs, new ministry ideas, big plans, and small groups. Look at what David said to Goliath and feel free to marvel at how specific he was. God hadn't given David specific instructions; David simply believed God would be with him, and he told Goliath what he was going to do and what would happen next. And speaking of David and Goliath . . . quit dreaming so small.

Third, emphasize the lordship of Christ in everything you do by emphasizing prayer. As a minister or leader, you have no authority unless you yourself are under the authority of Christ. Our elders meet every Monday morning for prayer, our women pray in between our worship services, and our church has held special nights for praise and prayer. The more we pray and the more fervently we pray, the more it seems God has blessed us. Likewise, when we have relied on ourselves and neglected prayer, things around here have suffered. Make every meeting of church leadership a spiritual event by recognizing that the real chairman of the board is sitting at the right hand of the Father and listening to you.

Finally, make it your goal to have a healthy church body. By that I mean a church and church leaders who understand why they are there, how evil sin is, and ways to display the humility and love Christ commands. Our church has struggled through many conflicts and offenses, and we know God commanded us to deal with such things. So we deal with them. You can't get any more like Christ than when you are teaching and demanding faith, righteousness, and love. Pray for wisdom as Solomon did, and believe you have received it just like Jesus said; then step out in faith like David did and begin to push, challenge, encourage, rebuke, and teach sound doctrine, just as Titus and Timothy were told to do. Not just from the pulpit, but all the time. Don't stop! Don't quit trying new things as you move toward the goal of building a healthy church. Whatever it takes, keep your efforts moving in the right direction. Teach your congregation to eat right (the Word), exercise (pursuing a vision), and avoid destructive behavior and junk food (false doctrine and sin). Healthy bodies grow.

CHAPTER SIX

TEAM MINISTRY:
ORGANIZING FOR EFFECTIVE SERVICE

MARK G. MAGEE

I AM THE SENIOR MINISTER of the Lewes Church of Christ in Milton, Delaware. I know most of you are thinking, "Del-a-where?" Delaware is the second smallest state in the union, on the east coast just south of Pennsylvania and east of Maryland. The state of Delaware is part of the DelMarVa Peninsula. Surrounded by the Atlantic Ocean and the Chesapeake Bay, the DelMarVa Peninsula is comprised of Delaware, a portion of Maryland, and a bit of Virginia. For the most part, the DelMarVa Peninsula is rural—the chicken capital of the world.

I grew up in southern Ohio and for all practical purposes the two locations are pretty much the same, except Delaware has a beach. In some senses, Delaware is secluded from the "mainland." People who come to Delaware don't bring their creativity, energy, or technology. They simply come to relax at the beach. Most come to our community to vacation. Because of our resort setting and our proximity to Washington D.C., Baltimore, and Philadelphia, we are known as the "Summer Capital of the World." Need a great place for a summer vacation? Come to Delaware and visit us at the Lewes Church of Christ on Coastal Highway just north of Lewes.

I became the preacher of this congregation in the summer of 1993. At the time our average attendance was 45. The congregation had been without a preacher for about a year, and the people were solid but exhausted. For nearly a year I had said, "No!" to their invitation to be their preacher. I wanted to move closer to home in southern Ohio. But the Lord had other plans. I agreed to be their preacher when the church agreed to break their traditional mold and become radically different for Christ (although I've learned since that not everyone wanted to be radically different for Christ).

During the last 13 years, we have successfully moved from a traditional to a relevant and contemporary approach to ministry. This has created some tension between our church and some surrounding churches that still prefer to do ministry with a 1950s flare. In my 13 years at Lewes, I've seen the Lord's blessing time and time again as the church has grown from 45 to more than 330. We are presently in a relocation project that allows us to meet in an auditorium that can seat 600 in one service. The Lord continues to bless.

The truth is, every church is important. Every Christian is a part of the body of Christ. Every congregation can accomplish God's purpose in its community. You don't have to be a megachurch to have mega impact on someone's faith, maturity, family, commitment, personal growth, or life transformation. In fact, we know all Heaven rejoices when just one comes to the Savior. Every church can get excited about that.

Principles and Strategies for Effective Ministry

Some churches are healthy and some are dysfunctional. Only a healthy church can reach its potential. Let's consider several areas of ministry needed for a church to achieve its potential.

Identity

One of the first things a smaller church must consider is its identity. Your identity helps answer questions like "Who are we?" and "What does the Lord want us to do?"

I grew up in a strong Christian family. I belonged to a church with a great youth group—in fact, in my graduating class of 48, 13 were Christians belonging to the youth group of which I was a part. We were the peer pressure. Then I went to Bible college, took a couple seminary classes, and jumped into an associate ministry position. It was there, in my mid-twenties, in the middle of ministry that I began to realize I was no longer living my parents' faith, nor was I a parrot repeating what I had been taught. I had to own my faith. I had to know what the Bible says for myself. I began to identify my identity.

The church at Lewes went through a similar process. During our monthly leadership meetings, we stopped talking about money for a new microphone, the grass cutting schedule, the color of the carpet, and whether or not it was OK for the preacher to take an extra day of vacation. We started asking other questions. What are our strengths? What are our weaknesses? What are our unique opportunities? What is our purpose as a church? What does God want us to do? We asked other questions as well. What really matters? Where will we stand? What will never change? What will we fight for? What will we die for?

Finding answers to those questions became paramount. We took more than two years to pray, study, and wrestle with these questions in order develop our purpose statement, mission statement, and our core values. Then, when we thought we had it, we'd tweak it again. But once we had these in place, we were able to proceed with focus.

Purpose

After several months—even years—of tweaking, we nailed down the specifics: Our purpose is "to please and to praise Jesus" (2 Corinthians 5:9). Our mission is "to inspire hope for life by connecting people to Jesus Christ and to one another." Our core values are the lordship of Jesus Christ, the worship of Almighty God, the fellowship of the church, and the discipleship of ourselves and others for the cause of Christ." We state our identity this way: "We are a contemporary style church mainly targeting families but having an appeal to all age groups. We are committed to bringing an inspirational, relevant message from the Word of God that can be easily applied in today's life. We incorporate state of the art audio and video technology in our services to help create an atmosphere of inspiration, challenge, and attraction for the Lord."

Vision

Our vision is a picture of where God wants us to be and what he wants us to accomplish. Vision is a portrait of where we know the Lord wants us to go, a snapshot of success. Vision helps people see the big picture. Vision helps people understand their part in the whole.

Leadership

Every church has leaders. Even when leaders are not formally set apart, someone in the group will begin to lead and influence others. Right now someone is leading your church. It may be for the good, or it may not be for the good. But someone is leading. Effective ministry requires having the right people in the right leadership positions. The church is the most important institution or organization in the universe. That being so, church leadership is the most important position in the world today. We believe that and take it seriously at LCC. We determined that we would raise the bar of church leadership. Early in our growth process we agreed that congregational oversight would not be left to amateurs on a part-time basis. Our basic criteria for leadership positions in our congregation is that they must be "F.A.T.": **F**aithful to the Word of God, **A**vailable to the Lord's leading, and **T**eachable—always on the grow.

Passion

Pray for passionate people. When you bring together people who are passionate about the Lord, passionate about his Word, and passionate about his people, you will find yourself on a great adventure. When you know who you are in the Lord and have an idea of what he wants you to do, and when you assign mature, passionate people to places of leadership, effective service will take place.

Philosophy

From our perspective, the mission of the church, illustrated by the shepherd and his flock, is to produce and mature sheep. Church leadership is all about maturing sheep. We have recently developed a leadership philosophy we call our "next step" philosophy. We continually ask what is our next step as a church. On a personal level we continue to focus on each person's next step in the faith. This requires relationship, evaluation, and direction.

Attitude

Some people say attitude is everything. Well, at least 99 percent. I grew up watching several churches who taught the right doctrine and engaged in good programs, but their attitudes were poor and negative. Most people really didn't care what they knew. Attitude is important. We are the people of God. We've been redeemed from sin and eternal destruction. We've been commissioned with the good news. That calls for smiles, joy, celebration, and positive moods. Our worship services, our Bible studies, and our marketplace interactions ought to be filled with joy. Check your attitude.

Commitments

We made some basic commitments early on that have allowed us to engage in effective ministry. It's not just a matter of what you do; it's about how you do it and why.

Our purpose is to glorify God in all we do. We've learned that when the Lord finds someone who will give him the glory and credit, he will continue to use that person or church for even greater glory. Our desire as a church is simply to make God famous.

Our direction comes from the Word of God. Everything we do must be rooted in Scripture. Passion for Scripture is a must. We study God's Word not only for information, but for transformation. The power of God is in the Word of God. It points us to Jesus and calls us to repentance. Often you will hear me begin a sermon (as I hold up my Bible), "This is my Bible. It points me to Jesus. I will trust and obey!"

Our efforts will be marked by excellence. We decided early that if we were going to do anything with Jesus' name attached to it, it deserved to be done with excellence. On one occasion while preaching from the Parable of the Talents (Matthew 25:14-30), I kept reading over Christ's statement, "Well done, good and faithful servant!" And it hit me. Would Jesus ever say, "Well done" if it really wasn't done well? No! He can't lie. Therefore, I committed to giving my best to him.

Our offerings as a church would be tithed. If the Lord promised to bless those who tithe on a personal basis, why wouldn't he bless the church that took the same challenge? Even when we were forty-five members strong, we committed to giving ten percent to help others, and we have never experienced financial stress.

Leadership requires full-time commitment and availability. Leadership is paramount, and it deserves our best people and our best effort. At LCC it is a full-time position. We refuse to treat it as a part-time position.

Obstacles

When you organize for effective ministry, you will face obstacles. Plenty of obstacles. Some of these obstacles will come from very good people. But never forget who the real enemy is. When you shake the shackles of mediocrity and get serious about effective ministry and influence for Jesus Christ, the devil will show up. He will use other churches, long time church members, and even your own family to thwart the momentum of God. But our experience has taught us that God never loses a battle he's been invited to fight.

Where to Go from Here

(1) Pray. No, this isn't a typical Sunday school cliché. Ask the Lord of the harvest to send forth workers. Nothing good and powerful will happen in the church unless it is the result of prayer.

(2) Set aside your monthly board meeting agenda, get out your Bibles, and begin to ask some hard questions about your church: Who are we? What does the Lord want us to do? In what must we succeed for Christ? What are our congregational strengths? What are our obvious weaknesses? In the scope of eternity, what really matters? (Note: this may take a long time!)

(3) After you know and are united around your identity, give yourself permission to take a "ministry fast." Stop everything, erase the board, start from scratch, and do only the things that matter and are effective. Get off the dead horses that are in your congregation. And yes, you have them. Don't be afraid to rethink everything, even basic doctrines. On a few occasions I found myself parroting bad doctrines I had been taught as a kid. ("Lord, forgive me.") Faith has to be personal and faith must be biblical.

(4) With focused identity, understood purpose, and clear vision, implement ministries that matter. Implement only those ministries that help you fulfill your mission, purpose, and vision. Start with just a few things—two or three—and do them well and grow from there.

(5) Once you begin or restart new ministries, evaluate everything. We constantly ask, "What was the best part about that . . . (sermon, service, program)?" and "What could we have done to make this even better?" Evaluate everything. Evaluate sermons, Sunday services, youth group events, elders meetings, bulletins, and music selection. It's the only way to achieve excellence. This constant evaluation will teach the necessity of change and prepare the church for seeing the positive side of change.

(6) Realize every team has to have one quarterback. For every ministry area, appoint one person who will oversee and give an account for that team. Again, leadership is paramount. I keep praying that God raises up the right leader in the right place at the right time. Leadership positions are not popularity contests. Leadership positions are for those who are mature in the faith, passionate about the ministry, gifted to carry it out, and responsible to see it through. Leadership in the church isn't about filling a position, but fulfilling a function. Your next round of leaders shouldn't be found in an election. Instead, watch and see who is already leading with a passion for the Lord.

(7) Acknowledge the Lord. As success becomes apparent and territory is captured for the Lord, keep glorifying him and making him famous. When the Lord finds someone or a group of someone's willing to give him the glory, credit, and honor, he will continue using that group to get more glory.

Action Steps

(1) Write into your weekly schedule a time simply to pray for effective ministry.

(2) Provide outside inspiration. Sometimes we forget that the world is quite big. Go to a convention, take a road trip to another church, invite an expert to your church to lead a seminar. There is nothing like inspiration from others who do it well to excite your people to exercise their own creativity.

(3) Use teaching opportunities within the church to explore issues of identity, purpose, mission, and vision. Don't just tell them what it is, explore it with them. You can easily do this in a smaller church. Explore the

foundations together. (Some of the Scriptures you may want to include in your exploration are: Matthew 5:13-16; 9:35; 11:28-30; 16:15-19; 18:19, 20; 22:36-40; 24:14; 25:34-40; 28:16-20; Mark 10:43-45; Luke 4:18, 19; 4:43-45; John 4:23; 10:14-18; 13:34, 35; 20:21; Acts 1:8; 2:41-47; 4:32-35; 6:1-7; Romans 12:1-8; 15:1-7; 1 Corinthians 12:12-31; 2 Corinthians 5:17–6:1; Galatians 5:13-15; 6:1, 2; Ephesians 1:22, 23; 2:19-22; 3:6; 3:14-21; 4:11-16; 5:23, 24; Colossians 1:24-28; 3:15, 16; 1 Thessalonians 1:3; 5:11; Hebrews 10:24, 25; 13:7; 1 Peter 2:9, 10; 1 John 1:5-7; 4:7-21.

(4) Create a list of core values or top priorities that will never change. We keep two lists of core values in our church. The first list deals with core value commitments of the leadership (some examples are: committed to the Word of God, committed to excellence, committed to raising the bar for church leadership, tithing every dime, and so on.) The second list concerns core values for the church. We want everyone committed to and actively involved in our four core values: the lordship of Jesus Christ, the worship of Almighty God, the fellowship of the church, and the discipleship of ourselves first and then others for the cause of Christ.

(5) Make following Christ an experience. Christianity isn't a ritualistic religion, but a living relationship with Jesus our Lord. Often in the church we've allowed form to drive function. Eventually the function aspect is lost, and we are left with a lifeless skeleton in the closet.

When a smaller congregation desires to make the Lord famous and when they develop leaders with passion for the Lord and for his people with the goal of hearing the Lord proclaim, "Well done!" effective ministry will happen. It's not about having the right skill set, but having the right mind-set. And when the Lord finds a F.A.T. man or woman (Faithful, Available, and Teachable), effective ministry will happen. May the Lord bless you and the congregation you serve with F.A.T. people for effective ministry. I know he wants to answer that prayer.

CHAPTER SEVEN

CONFLICT MANAGEMENT:
MAINTAINING UNITY THROUGH
PREVENTION, INTERVENTION, AND RESOLUTION

BARNEY WELLS

TO LIVE ABOVE
With the saints we love,
Ah, that will be glory.
To live below
With the ones we know,
That's a different story.

Many preachers have quoted that little poem over the years, and most of us understand its sentiment. While it certainly is pleasant for brothers to "live together in unity" (Psalm 133:1), it seems inevitable that they will sometimes live in conflict. This chapter shares some of what one smaller rural church has learned about preventing, intervening in, and resolving conflict.

Since 1889, the Walnut Grove Christian Church has met in a traditional white-frame building at a country crossroads about five miles southeast of Arcola, Illinois. The flat prairie surrounding the church house for miles is some of the most productive farmland in the nation. Sitting on the eastern edge of Illinois' largest Amish settlement, the community has a living link to its past. Its ever-growing Hispanic population, Interstate highway exit, and industrial park point to its future. For most of its history, Arcola has existed to serve the needs of the area farmers, and the community's churches, including Walnut Grove, have been made up of those same farmers. In the last twenty years, however, Arcola has changed. As the size of farms has increased, the number of resident farmers has declined. More of the residents are professionals, factory workers, and folk who commute to office jobs a half-hour or more away.

Over the decades the Walnut Grove congregation has seen many changes, including the complete demolition and reconstruction of its building and a merger with an a cappella Church of Christ. The pace of change accelerated as the 21st century approached, and the congregation added first part-time and then full-time staff, completed two building additions, added a second worship service, and changed its system of governance, completely rewriting its bylaws. In a fifteen-year period from 1990-2005, the congregation made just about every kind of change a church can make. In that same period, some changes came to the congregation that were neither intended nor desired. Two major area employers closed, some key church leaders moved away due to job relocations, and a couple of wise and faithful elders passed away. Throughout this period the church was growing, and that meant change.

Change Can Bring Conflict

Unlike other chapters in this book, this chapter is not about any one particular change or plan or program; rather it is about what the leadership at Walnut Grove learned about managing conflict during a decade and a half of almost constant change. The potential for conflict is always present in a church and can be triggered either by change or by a failure to change when change is needed. For the smaller church to release its power, it is going to have to implement deliberate changes and respond to unexpected changes in its context. To safely navigate the waters of change, you can't rock the boat too much.

"I'm all for progress; it's *change* I don't like." That statement points to one of the reasons change can bring conflict—some members may not see its purpose. Everyone makes change. We change the car we drive every few years, we change the clothes we wear, and we change the restaurants where we like to eat. When we see how a change will benefit us, we call it progress and we embrace it. It is when we don't see the potential benefit in a change or see that it may bring difficulties for us even if it benefits the church as a whole that we may resist change. No one wants to see his church make a change that isn't progress, so it is not unexpected that good Christian folks will resist changes in which they see no benefit. That may bring them into conflict with folks in the church who do see benefits to the change. Effective leadership in the smaller church requires we understand this need to see the change as progress.

Just as people may not see the same benefit from a change, they may not accept the change at the same pace. For over forty years, Everett M. Rogers has studied the way people accept change. In *Diffusion of Innovations* (The Free Press, 1995), Rogers has observed that only about 2.5 percent of people in any group (like a church congregation) ever have a new idea. Once they have it, about 13.5 percent more will see the value in it right away. A third of the people in the group will accept the idea after watching it work for a while, and another third will slowly accept the idea. That leaves about sixteen percent who will never really accept it. A few of those will leave the group rather than make the change. Rogers' research confirms for the church leader that it will be the rare change that does not produce some conflict.

Sometimes, no matter how hard leaders may try to anticipate all the results of a change, things may happen that no one predicted or planned. This is called the Law of Unintended Consequences. One change Walnut Grove made, in preparation for the larger change of starting a second worship service, was a very simple one—from glass communion cups to disposable plastic cups. All the groups within the church who had any stake in the change had agreed it was a good one, and we were all looking forward to it. On our first Sunday with plastic cups, before the tray had passed six pews, one arthritic old brother had crushed the cup, splashing his Sunday white shirt with grape juice, and another dear old saint had cut her lip on a tiny bit of flash where the cup had come from the mold. At the conclusion of the service the plastic cups disappeared and have never since been used. The congregation hoped to accomplish several worthwhile goals in the change, but none of them involved the embarrassment and injury of two senior members. These were good-natured and loving souls who did not complain, but under different circumstances these unintended consequences could have led to conflict.

Our experience with change at Walnut Grove and the research done by others confirm that change can bring conflict, and yet we managed to negotiate most of our changes with very little conflict in the church. The following sections describe what we learned about preventing, intervening in, and resolving conflict resulting from change.

Prevention of Conflict

The New Testament calls for us to be of one mind (Roman 12:5; 15:5, 6; 1 Corinthians 12:11; Philippians 1:27; 2:2; 1 Peter 3:8) and insists we be united on issues that touch salvation. Yet even in the early church we see evidence that not everyone, even good Christians, thought alike about everything. Just as our tastes in food or our style of shoes may differ because of the way we are raised, so there are some things about how we view the world that may vary with our upbringing and environment. These are not things that are right or wrong; they are simply different ways of doing the same thing. As mentioned, one of the changes Walnut Grove experienced was a shift in occupation base. The farm crisis of the 80s left the community and the church with fewer farmers, yet the church continued to grow, attracting newcomers to the community who lacked the agrarian roots of the long-time members. In order to prevent conflict, we had to learn that some folks thought differently about things, and that was not a bad thing. Here are some examples.

In the last fifteen years the Walnut Grove congregation has been involved in two building programs, one of them in two phases. One of the first questions that comes up in a smaller church, especially a rural one, is volunteer labor. Agrarians, folks raised with the rhythms of the land, tend to be do-it-yourself folks. Being their own boss, they typically feel they have more time to give than money. They try not to hire anything done if they can do it, and that mind-set is often applied to church building projects. They also have a view of time that is conditioned by their work. Time is based more on events than on clocks or calendars, so they will plan a project for "after planting," or "when the tourist season is over." On the other hand, there are those folks coming to the church who grew up in a suburban culture, work in offices, factories, or schools, and plan their schedules very tightly. They view work as a specialization: you do what you are good at and outsource the rest to specialists in other areas. Neither of these ways of looking at time and work are wrong, and neither is more biblical than the other; but each can seem foreign and foolish to those who do not hold them.

This came home to us in a big way when we started our second building project. During our first project we had done everything we could with volunteer labor, paying only for work that required a license or a skill no one in the church possessed. When the decision was made on the second project, the make-up of the church had changed considerably and the board voted unanimously to make this addition a "turn-key" operation, hiring the entire job done by a contractor. The first day the contractor came to start work, several volunteers also showed up, asking how they could help. They came back the next day and finally the contractor suggested that he just do the parts that required special skills and tools and leave the rest to the volunteers. Some of those volunteers were the same people who voted to hire out the whole job. We (I was one of them) just couldn't shake the mind-set, even though we realized the value in doing it a different way.

Another area where we found differing mind-sets we call "margins." Agrarians, especially farmers, live with a great deal of risk, always investing most of their profits (sometimes more than all their profit) in next year's crop. They live with the possibility that the growing season can be too wet or too dry, too hot or too cold, there can be wind and hail and insects and . . . suffice it to say they always see a high degree of risk and a low amount of liquid assets in their business. This makes them very sensitive to having their church take risks as well. On the other hand, those whose business resources are supplied by the home office and whose assets are more liquid do not feel the same degree of risk and therefore are more comfortable with their church taking a bigger "step of faith." Neither of these groups lacks faith, but one sees faith in God focused in what their business undertakes, while the other sees it focused in what their church undertakes. Again, this difference can result in accusations of "little faith" or "foolhardiness," which in turn can lead to conflict, if leaders do not realize the validity of both positions.

Church members can also hold different mind-sets in the way they view other people. Smaller churches, especially rural ones, tend to view people in terms of relationships, while relative newcomers may view people by their roles. The latter may identify a person as "one of our elders, an attorney, and on the county planning commission," while the former may identify the same man as "Bob, Doc and Vera's boy; lives on the old Helms place." The first group may tend to ignore the role of a church leader because of the person's relationships, and the second may overlook how relationships affect how one carries out his role. Either can lead to conflict, yet neither is inherently wrong.

To sum this up, we at Walnut Grove learned that while we may be of one mind about what to do, we may have differing ideas about how to do it, and all of those ideas may be good ones. To help prevent conflict, church leaders must recognize that their mind-set may not represent the only, or even the best way to accomplish a project. Having recognized this, they need to help others see the value of doing a task in a different way, valuing what a different mind-set may bring to the project. This task of helping each group see the validity of the other's thinking and helping them work together to bring out the best of both will help prevent conflicts.

Theological Preparation

The church is different from any other organization in that it is the body and the bride of Christ, the only organization designed and created by God. Therefore anything the church does is essentially theological. If we want to avoid conflict, our first question should be, "What does God want us to do?" Seeking that guidance from God begins in prayer. One may think it goes without saying that a congregation would pray about the decisions it makes, but unfortunately what goes without saying also often goes without doing.

When Jesus had a decision to make, such as choosing the Twelve, he spent the night in prayer (Luke 6:12). When the church in Antioch wanted to undertake a new ministry, the leaders spent considerable time in prayer and fasting (Acts 13:1-3). We have found at Walnut Grove that the more time we spend in prayer about what to do and how to do it, the better things work out. This prayer for direction is not just the work of the leadership. Involving the entire congregation in praying for God's guidance gives everyone a heart to hear his answer and makes conflict less likely.

In Matthew 5:37 Jesus tells us to let our "Yes" be yes and our "No" be no. His injunction against taking oaths is also good advice for making conflict-free decisions in the local church. Starting with our first building project at Walnut Grove, we learned that sometimes an elder or board member may give assent to a decision in a meeting, but then reverse the position when confronted by a church member who disagrees with or misunderstands the decision. This is a recipe for conflict. A church cannot be unified if its leaders are not unified. There may be discussion and even argument in a meeting, but once a decision is reached, the leaders should speak with one voice. We have found it helpful to make the final decision by a roll-call vote, where each leader goes on record as supporting the decision. When questions or objections from members of the church arise, each leader should be willing and able to explain why he supports the decision. It is nearly impossible to have a unified church without a unified leadership.

When a major decision or change faces a congregation, the leadership may and should study the Scripture in order to reach a biblically informed conclusion. The leaders may feel they have good biblical reasons for the decision they make, yet forget that the congregation has not gone through the same study. Conflict can be prevented by sermons that prepare the congregation to think theologically about the change that may be coming. At Walnut Grove, before we began our second Sunday morning service and before we changed our Sunday morning format, several sermons over a period of more than a year dealt with topics that helped the congregation build a theology of the church gathered. The sermons looked at questions about what could change and could not, addressed issues and attitudes, and presented the same Scriptures the leaders had been studying. Don't wait until the last two or three weeks before a change and then rush in a barrage of sermons. Treat the topic as it comes up in the normal course of preaching through a book or series over several months. The bigger the change, the further in advance you should start preaching about the issues involved. Conflict can be prevented by making sure the entire congregation understands the biblical basis behind a change the church is making.

Persuasive Presentations

In the middle of the 20th century, the USDA undertook one of the grandest efforts at mass change ever attempted. They set out to convince the nation's corn farmers to switch from planting open-pollinated corn to hybrid seed corn. To accomplish this task they trained an army of "county agents" and sent them into corn producing counties. These county agents had been trained to know all the benefits of hybrid seed and effective methods for growing the corn. They could explain every reason a farmer should switch, but just by talking they could only convince a few. Then they hit on an idea. Instead of trying to persuade the remaining farmers, they simply waited until after harvest, and took them to visit the farms of the few who had planted the new hybrid seed. Those farmers were delighted with the results, and their reports of success were far more persuasive than anything the county agent could say. By bringing together those who needed to make a change and those who had successfully made it, the agents greatly increased the acceptance of the new idea.

At Walnut Grove, the same principle worked. When we were considering adding a second service, we talked with other churches like us who had already made the change. When we were considering adding an elevator to our building, we did the same thing. Hearing the satisfaction and encouragement of those like us who had done what we were considering significantly reduced the level of anxiety, and therefore the possibility of conflict.

"A word aptly spoken is like apples of gold in settings of silver" (Proverbs 25:11). Sometimes, when a situation holds real potential for conflict, a brief word aptly spoken can bring things together. Such a situation existed at Walnut Grove Christian Church as the congregation met to vote on a proposed building addition.

The leadership had all endorsed the plan to build, but the $80,000 price tag was the biggest thing the church had ever attempted, and as the congregation met, the outcome of the meeting was in doubt. Throughout the meeting some spoke in favor of adding the educational wing while others expressed considerable reservations about the project. For over an hour the discussion flowed back and forth, with no real consensus. Then Mary Katherine spoke.

Mary Katherine was in her 70s, retired from her job as a nurse in the town doctor's office. She didn't make it to church much because on Sunday mornings she looked after her aged mother and aunt so their regular caregiver could take the day off. She hadn't come to a congregational meeting in over a decade, but this night she came. She always carried a bag of yarn and crochet hooks, and during all the discussion she sat quietly crocheting. When the discussion tapered off and it seemed there was nothing else to say and the issue still seemed very much undecided, Mary Katherine laid aside her yarn and hooks, stood up, and said, "I don't get to church as much as I used to, and I don't teach Sunday school any more, but I've taught a lot of you, and we need these classrooms." She sat back down and resumed her crocheting. The proposition to build passed unanimously.

You cannot arrange for people like Mary Katherine to speak. God will raise them up when needed. There are in every congregation those who seem to be peacemakers, ambassadors to a certain age group or constituency of the church, who can smooth ruffled feathers and explain positions in ways that most cannot. Rarely is the preacher one of these people; nor will most of the elders fill this role. But these people are there by God's design, and they are of great value in preventing conflict.

Intervention in Conflict

No matter how careful church leaders may be to prevent conflict, it will still happen from time to time. It may arise within the church, as a reaction to decisions the leaders have made or to an inappropriate and unsanctioned action by some church member. It may also come into the church from the outside, as a result of business or family conflicts between two or more church households. Usually such conflict is so quietly held and quickly resolved the leaders never know about it. Now and then, however, every church will experience the kind of conflict where the resolution does not come about quickly and spontaneously. The conflict remains and may even grow. Those situations require intervention.

While not specifically about intervention in church conflict, Matthew 5:21-24 and 18:15-17 provide a good framework for conflict intervention. Here are some principles for conflict intervention we have learned from these passages.

Do it now! When a conflict in the church requires intervention, don't wait. The sooner the intervention takes place, the less damage the conflict will do. It is a natural human tendency to avoid conflict situations. Most church leaders don't want to be involved in conflict, so we tend to look the other way and hope the conflict goes away on its own. It rarely does. An early intervention has the best chance of success and results in the least amount of emotional baggage.

Keep the discussions focused on issues, not people or personalities. Each party in a church conflict may see the other as a "fool" or evil, or both. Rarely is either the case. Sometimes either or both parties may misapply Scripture to support their case, thereby enhancing the "evil" status of the other party. Near the end of the Cold War, one small congregation was conflicted about the morality of smuggling Bibles into the Soviet Union. One of the pro-smuggling group cited Paul's escape from Damascus by being "smuggled" out in a basket as scriptural proof that God was on the pro-smuggling side. He may have been, but that passage didn't prove it. By encouraging conflicted church members to focus on the issues and respect each other as believers who are loved by Christ, relationships can be restored and maintained while issues are resolved. Sometimes just valuing the individual resolves the issue.

Involve as few people as possible in the intervention. Matthew 18 says it is best if only the people actually conflicted are involved. As soon as they realize a conflict exists, they should work it out. If they did so, no intervention would be needed. Again our natural tendencies get in the way of our Christian life. When a church leader becomes aware that one member has a conflict with another, the first response should be to encourage the two to talk and involve no one else. What often happens, however, is that the leader contacts a few other leaders and soon there is much concern but no action toward reconciliation. The farther the story of the conflict spreads, the more distorted it becomes, the more people take one side or the other, and the harder it is to resolve. If the parties in conflict will not or cannot work through the issue themselves, it may be necessary to mediate. Again, involve no more in this process than it takes to get the job done.

Conflicts happen between real people, brothers and sisters in Christ. One of the first and best decisions the elders at Walnut Grove made in regard to conflict intervention was that "'Somebody' doesn't go to church here." Anonymous complaints were not brought to meetings. If someone has an issue with a person, action, or decision, the elders are glad to listen, but the "someone" has to be named. We cannot resolve conflicts with unnamed parties. These are our brothers and sisters in Christ. If there is a conflict with one or more of them, we should deal with it personally, and we can only do that if the person has a name.

No matter how hard you work to prevent conflict, it will come. Expect it. Prepare for it. When it comes, intervene quickly and with as few people as possible.

Resolution of Conflict

You may notice that much space was given to preventing conflict, less space to intervening, and less still here to resolution. That is because if you work well at preventing it, you won't need to intervene often, and if you intervene promptly, resolution will naturally follow—most of the time. Most church members really do not want conflict in their lives or in the church, and given a little help and encouragement will resolve their conflicts in short order. Now and then, however, amicable resolution doesn't come. Then the leaders must take a different kind of action.

Matthew 18:17 shows that some conflicts must be addressed by the leadership church-wide, and sometimes individuals must be allowed, or even required, to leave. Earlier we said that those involved in church conflicts are rarely evil, but once in a while they are. John speaks of such a circumstance in 3 John 9, 10, and Paul warns the Ephesian elders that some of their own number would distort the truth and split the church (Acts 20:30). To resolve conflict in such situations requires the leaders to take a united, firm, and public stand against anyone who is damaging the church and will not accept correction.

Even in a forceful and unpleasant resolution of conflict there is hope. Paul and Barnabas parted company because of Paul's distrust of Mark, yet years later Paul testified to Mark's value in ministry. A disruptive and unrepentant member of the Corinthian congregation was put out of the church, yet was later restored (2 Corinthians 2:5-8). When a disruptive member does not repent and return, the overall health of the congregation is still strengthened by the removal of the conflict.

There is no question that even the congregations we read about in the New Testament had some conflict. We should not be surprised if our congregation does as well. We would not want to leave the impression that we have always handled conflict perfectly at Walnut Grove, but when we have followed the principles set forth here, our times of conflict have been brief and unity quickly restored.

CHAPTER EIGHT

SUNDAY SCHOOLS AND SMALL GROUPS:
TEACHING GOD'S WORD WITH PURPOSE

ERIC BINGAMAN

I T'S HARD FOR ME TO EXPLAIN WHAT I AM FEELING," Shirley confided in me one afternoon, "but I just don't feel connected." I had only been at the rural Kentucky church for a couple of months, and this was my first experience as the only paid staff member of a smaller congregation. I remember vividly how taken aback I was by her statement. All I could offer was a weak, "Just give the relationships more time to develop" response.

It has been years since Shirley expressed her disappointment over her relationships within the church. I would not be surprised if she has since forgotten the conversation we had in the church fellowship hall of that small Kentucky river town. The questions raised that day forced me to reconsider everything I had ever been taught about community in the smaller church.

Like most, I was raised in a smaller church and have always served in a smaller church. It was instilled in me from a very early age that the small church was the small group. The culture of the smaller church has always supported the idea that it is the community that develops within these congregations that makes them special. Shirley's words that day communicated something different to me. Before she moved to Kentucky and joined our congregation (we averaged about forty on a good Sunday morning), Shirley belonged to a church that averaged more than 1,800 worshipers weekly. For the next hour she continued to tell me about the close community she had experienced in this large congregation but was not finding in this church of forty.

How could this be? The caring that takes place in the smaller church is what makes it unique, isn't it? Shirley was not one of those members who filled a pew on Sunday and was not heard from again until the following Sunday. She was an active participant in the life of the church and God's answer to many of my prayers. Shirley took care of the bulletins, helped mow the grass, was involved in the choir, and invited members over for dinner. She tried all the normal avenues one might use to get connected in a congregation, but despite her involvement in the church, it was the community that she found in a large congregation that she desired and could not find in this smaller body. Our conversation sparked my search and exploration for community and, ultimately, the role of small groups in the smaller church.

Our Story

The search that began in Kentucky led me to the Batesville Christian Church in Indiana. While much larger than that small river town in Kentucky, Batesville is still considered a smaller community with approximately 6,000 residents. Every community features certain traits that make it unique to the area, and Batesville is no different. However one trait affects every aspect of life and ministry in Batesville. Our community is the world headquarters for two large international corporations. These corporations bring a great deal of resources to the community and over time, have transformed her from a rural town living off the lumber industry to a rural, upper-middle class, white collar business community. These corporations have drawn many families from large metropolitan areas, leaving Batesville with an odd mix of rural, suburban, and urban values.

The Batesville Christian Church mirrors many of the same traits as the city in which it ministers. The church was founded more than thirty years ago by a local church planting organization. Through the years the church has grown from a congregation of a few local residents to a regional church made up of individuals from all walks of life and cities from across southeast Indiana. In describing the church's growth pattern over the years, one could only use the phrase *slow and steady*. There have never been great gains, losses, or plateaus in the weekly worship attendance. At her first Sunday service, the preacher rose to the pulpit to speak to one family. Today we have around 200 in attendance during our two morning services.

Many of our new members come from larger churches in metropolitan cities. Upon joining the church they came down with what may be called the "Shirley Syndrome." Like Shirley back in Kentucky, these individuals came into the smaller church after attending larger congregations. They immediately became involved in ministry. They played on the softball team, attended church events, and often invited members over for dinner. They were doing the customary activities we often suggest to newer members when trying to connect them to the life of the church. Despite their efforts, however, many still did not feel connected to the church body.

So we began our search into community and small groups. As you begin to think through what a small groups ministry may look like in your congregation, many questions will to come to mind. There are not enough pages in one chapter to explore all of these questions or describe the working model we have used at the Batesville Christian Church in detail. But I will address three of the most important questions we worked through while forming our working model and share some of our stories. In exploring these questions, it is my prayer that you will be challenged to rethink community and begin to dream about what a small groups ministry may look like in your community.

What is a small group?

Do you have children? Do you remember how easy parenting was going to be before you actually had those children? This past summer we took a trip to Williamsburg, Virginia. While I was coming out of one of the exhibits, I could hear my wife and our two-year-old, the youngest of three, in the distance. Mak had decided to have one of her two-year-old moments. I had to laugh as the young newlywed couple in front of me discussed how their children would never behave in such a manner. It was obvious neither of them had spent much time with a two-year-old who had been worn down from a week's worth of traveling—in addition to being an hour past lunch and nap time. As I grinned at their statement, I began to wonder how many times I had made that same comment when Shannon and I were first married. Before I became a parent, I had the answers to every parenting issue. Then the day comes when that child is suddenly in your home at 2:00 AM and will not stop crying no matter what you do. When you become a parent, you quickly realize how little you know.

We were in a similar situation with our small groups ministry. Deciding to begin a small groups ministry was easy, but now what? How do we go about placing a small groups ministry together? We had fallen into the trap of believing small groups were a fad for larger churches that would soon be gone. Now we found ourselves seeing the need for such a ministry in the smaller church.

While I am certain there are hundreds of smaller churches across the country successfully implementing small groups in their community, we did not know where they were or what models they were using. So we began our search for community by studying the early church.

In searching the pages of Scripture, we discovered simple, age-old practices often overlooked in our American model of the smaller church. When you think of "doing church," what image comes to mind? In our culture, we tend to think of "doing church" as corporate gatherings that occur once a week on Sunday morning. Attendance at these gatherings vary greatly, but could range anywhere from 20 to 20,000. As we looked through the Scriptures, we began to notice that in the wake of Paul's missionary journeys, house churches sprang up across the region (1 Corinthians 16:19; Philemon 2; Romans 16:3-5; Colossians 4:15). While Paul certainly suggests a distinction between house churches and the church as a whole (1 Corinthians 14:23; Romans 16:23), Luke describes in Acts 2:46 that the believers meet in the temple and in one another's homes. He also describes what took place in those home meetings. As they gathered in one another's homes, they prayed for one another (Acts 2:42; 12:12), they fellowshiped with one another (Acts 2:42), they observed Communion with one another (Acts 2:42), they shared the mission of evangelism with one another (Act 2:47), they worshiped together (Acts 2:47), they studied the teachings of Scripture with one another (Acts 2:42; 5:42), they cared for one another (Acts 2:45), they attended larger corporate gatherings together (Acts 2:46), and ultimately, they shared their lives with one another (Acts 2:46). Luke gives us an image of a small group of believers meeting together regularly in each other's homes fulfilling every "one another" command found in

Scripture. This should come as no surprise to us. Every "one another" command found in Scripture was first modeled by Jesus in a small group.

Some in smaller churches believe that because they know the names, employers, addresses, and latest community gossip related to those involved in the church, they have an intimate relationship with them. Scripture teaches us that the family of God should be so much more! Think about those relationships for a moment. Do you really know what goes on in the homes of the members of your church? Do you know what makes them cry? What keeps them up at night? Would they feel secure enough in your relationship to call you in the middle of the night and confess their deepest secrets?

Study the "one another" commands in Scripture. Are they being fulfilled in the way God intended? For the vast majority of us, I'm guessing the answer is no. It is often too easy for us to wear our Sunday masks, go to church, listen to the preacher, stand in the lobby discussing the weather, and return home without ever having to reveal what is really going on in our lives. As we began to formulate our plan for small groups, we intentionally set out to create an atmosphere where these masks would be removed and God's children could live life with one another in the type of community we find in the pages of Acts. So in answering the question "What is a small group?" we determined that our groups would be made up of individuals who volunteer intentionally to come together regularly and at a specific time for Bible study accompanied by practical application, fellowship, prayer, and Christian service. In other words, this is where we saw the life of the congregation being lived out. To convey this concept to the congregation, we called our small groups "Life Groups."

What will a small group meeting look like?

Carving pumpkins has become way too difficult! I remember the good old days when you just dug in and created whatever came to mind at the moment. Pumpkin carving has now become an art that requires patience and planning. One fall I surfed the Internet with my children and was amazed at the designs we could choose from. There was the "Scooby Doo" pumpkin, the "George Bush" pumpkin, the "Bob Hope" pumpkin, the "Casper" pumpkin, religious pumpkins, scary pumpkins, and funny pumpkins. There were more patterns than you could possibly imagine. There were so many designs that my oldest decided it would be easier to create a pumpkin face on his own rather than choose from the plethora of designs we were combing through on the Internet. As we discussed pumpkin carving with our children, we first had to go back and decide what we hoped to accomplish. We knew there were certain messages we did not want to communicate to our neighbors, so those designs were tossed. There were also designs that seemed too silly to consider, like the "John Wayne" pumpkin, so those designs were eliminated. As we began to better understand what we hoped to accomplish and communicate, we were better able to determine how we would shape our pumpkins.

Pick up any book on small groups and you will find a number of models for building your small group meetings. Before you determine what your small group meeting will look like, you need first to determine what you hope to accomplish in these meetings. As we studied the small groups of believers in the pages of the New Testament, we determined there were four goals we wanted to accomplish in our small groups. In the course of a year we wanted each of our groups to engage in Bible study, fellowship, prayer, and Christian service. We brought these goals into our mission statement: "Our mission is to build biblical community by connecting people into groups of six to twelve individuals who intentionally come together on a regular basis to grow closer to God and share in one another's lives."

Bible Study

At a conference I attended, one of the main session speakers mentioned in his message that his small group was his softball team. Later in our workshop discussions several asked about this illustration. In discussions with other attendees later on, I was faced with a question from a young lay leader who was confused about the definition of a small group. Can a softball team be a small group? Good question! That depends on the goals you hope to accomplish in your small groups ministry. In the model we have chosen for our ministry, we want our small groups to "devote themselves to the apostles' teaching" (Acts 2:42). This does not mean that every meeting is a Bible study. In fact, I encourage our groups to take a meeting every now and then to do something fun and grow closer together relationally. However, the majority of the time when they come together, these groups take thirty minutes of a ninety-minute meeting to study the Scriptures. The studies that occur during those thirty minutes have two essential components. They are first of all practical and heavy in application. At the Batesville Christian Church, we offer opportunities for heavy Bible study on Wednesday nights, in Sunday school, and during our worship services. Our goal for these groups is to take that knowledge and put it into practice while holding one another accountable. The second component comes out of the first. These studies are low on lecture and heavy on discussion. We train and equip our leaders to ask questions in an intentional manner that will make a point, yet draw out what is going on in the lives of their members. So can a softball team become a small group? In the model we are using, it could, but that team would need to come together for regular Bible study in addition to accomplishing fellowship, prayer, and Christian service.

Fellowship

What do you think of when you hear the word *fellowship*? Those of us who grew up in the smaller church may think of potluck dinners following the Sunday service. To some degree those dinners fulfill the Bible's call to fellowship with one another. When the New Testament writers used the Greek word *koinonia*, however, they had in mind a fellowship that was much more intimate than a couple of potlucks every year. The relationships we see in the pages of Scripture were so deep and sincere that Christians were willing to sell "their possessions and goods" and give "to anyone as he had need" (Acts 2:45). We wanted to create an atmosphere where the members of our small groups could pour their lives into one another. Two segments in every small group meeting help facilitate this goal. The first ten to fifteen-minutes of each meeting make up what I call warm up and re-entry. This is an informal segment where members enjoy refreshments and catch up on the events of the past week. In addition to this re-entry segment, we have a more formal segment of sharing time. In this fifteen to twenty-minute segment, our leaders will ask questions or lead group members in creative exercises designed to stir conversation about what is going on in one another's lives. While these questions and exercises are usually tied into the evening lesson, they help us take off our masks and open our lives to one another. A number of resources currently on the market provide examples of these types of exercises.

Prayer

If you had the ability to speak with the Almighty God one-on-one, what kind of conversation would you have with him? Would you stand in awe of his presence and offer up praise? Would you pour out your fears, questions, and hurts to him looking for guidance? Maybe you would take the opportunity to speak on behalf of a sick or hurting loved one. Too often we speak of the discussions we would like to have with God in the future tense. Through the Holy Spirit, we have that opportunity right now! Like many smaller churches, we offer a time before meetings and Sunday school for prayer. We still read prayer requests during our worship service and someone comes forward to offer a quick "Lord, I don't know all those who were mentioned, but you do and I give them to you" type of prayer.

So where does intimate prayer take place in the life of our congregation? In our small groups. In each meeting our groups are encouraged to take fifteen to twenty minutes for prayer. During our training sessions with small group leaders, we discuss different types of prayers and different models we can use. We teach our leaders not to offer quick prayers in order to move on to the next agenda item. Instead these leaders spend time going to God with their groups, praising him and lifting up their petitions by name. Most importantly, we empower and encourage our leaders to drop the entire night's agenda when a crisis occurs and use that time to go to God in prayer.

Christian Service

If your church suddenly disappeared, would the people in your community care? When my wife and I first interviewed at the Batesville Christian Church, we began to ask people in the community to give us their impressions of the church. Their responses were revealing. Their impressions were neither negative nor positive. Not one person in this community of 6,000 to whom we spoke had heard of the church. It seemed that if the church shut down, no one would notice. So we have become more intentional about leaving the security of our church building and getting involved in the life of the community.

One of the ways we are doing this is through our small groups ministry. We encourage our small groups to take on at least one community project during the year. Most of our small groups do much more. Our groups have served in the local battered women's shelter, adopted families in need, and held church services in nursing homes. These groups are serving all across the southeast Indiana region, and while our efforts have only begun, in the past year or two we have seen dramatic results. When we first began calling community organizations to help, they were somewhat hesitant. There is great fear in the unknown, and these organizations do not often receive calls saying "I have twelve people who want to help. How can you use them?" No longer do we have to make such calls. Many of the organizations in our community now know who we are and have developed enough trust to call us and ask if we can help out. Through our small groups and other outreach efforts, the community now knows who we are, and they know they can turn to us in times of crisis.

A Summary

Let me take a minute to review the structure of our small group meetings. Our weekly small group meetings last about ninety-minutes. This time is broken down into four segments. The first segment is our warm up and re-entry segment. This is an informal ten to fifteen-minute period at the beginning of a meeting where members informally catch up on the week's activities around refreshments. The second segment is a thirty to forty-five minute Bible study built around discussion with an emphasis on practical application. The third segment lasts fifteen to twenty minutes. During this time our groups participate in creative exercises designed to help members open up to one another. The final fifteen to twenty minute segment is devoted to prayer. No meeting is the same. Leaders are encouraged to move each segment around and to be creative in their approach. Occasionally meetings are canceled to have a picnic, go bowling, or serve in the community. All gatherings, regardless of their look, are designed to help members grow closer to God and to one another.

Where does Sunday school fit in?

Like many smaller churches across America, the Batesville Christian Church offers a traditional Sunday school ministry, holding two worship services with seven children's classes and three adult classes meeting in between. When we began building our small groups ministry, we did not consider how our traditional Sunday school ministry was going to fit into the church's overall plan. After our first year of small groups we noticed a number of individuals within our congregation were searching for community but were not ready for the intimacy of a small group. As we considered this it became clear that our Sunday school classes met this need.

As new members are assimilated into the life of the congregation, our first goal is to plug them into a small group. We used to focus on finding specific ministries for newcomers. But we concluded that people do not stay with our church because they have a job. They stay because they have become part of the life of the congregation.

This was certainly true of Jenny and John (whose names I have changed). When Jenny and John moved to Batesville, they visited our congregation and fell in love with our church family. As they continued to grow and became better acquainted with our congregation and beliefs, they began to realize our congregation came from a different tradition than what they were familiar with and had known most of their lives. Other churches in our area were more representative of their tradition, and they continued to look at them. That was until several months ago, when they came forward and became members of our church family. In talking with them later, I learned that while they enjoyed our worship services, something else caused them to stay with our congregation. Their small group had become their family. They could have easily left our corporate body to join a church from a familiar tradition. What they couldn't do was break the relationships they had built in their small group.

So our primary goal is to move members directly into a small group. Those who are not yet ready for that intimacy are plugged into a mid-size group such as the Sunday school. Relationships can begin there until members feel comfortable enough to join a small group. Our adult classes are taught by small group leaders. Because our small group leaders are also our Sunday school teachers, their small group activities frequently surface as illustrations in their teaching, which reinforces the concept of community we have for all believers, encouraging others to take part in this ministry.

Our exploration into community has changed us, challenged us, and drawn us closer to God and to each other. What does community look like in the life of your church family? I believe some sort of small group ministry is needed in every church family regardless of size. The look of that ministry may be different from community to community, but the impact will remain the same. In such a ministry you will find a community of believers growing closer to each other and to God in a way few believed they would ever see but always dreamed of.

CHAPTER NINE

MEN'S MINISTRIES:
REACHING, TEACHING, AND MENTORING MEN

BILL BUTTERFIELD

WILLIAMSBURG, JAMESTOWN, AND YORKTOWN, VIRGINIA . . . the Historic Triangle! Four hundred years ago in 1607, explorers landed at what is now known as Jamestown, Virginia. From that moment there has been a continuous habitation of this historic area. Hundreds of thousands of people visit Williamsburg every year to drink from history's fountain. *Money* magazine recently listed Williamsburg as one of the top five retirement areas in the United States. Recreational opportunities abound. But more importantly Williamsburg is home to 12,000 people. The stream of people from "sea to shining sea" winding their way to Williamsburg is steadily increasing. The future of this historic village is as bright as its glorious past.

Too often those of us who call Williamsburg home find ourselves wanting to protect it from further expansion because we do not want to lose the "down home" uniqueness of the area. Some would say we have more than enough restaurants, hotels, and businesses, but others welcome the possibilities each new venture presents. Families live in affluent neighborhoods less than a mile from streets lined with low income housing. Service jobs are plentiful along with multiple opportunities for career advancement.

Williamsburg is home to four high schools and the College of William and Mary with its enviable academic reputation. The military is well represented as every branch of the service operates a base within a radius of ten miles of our community. Our military bases bring in young families from various cultures adding to the uniqueness of our town. This is Williamsburg, Virginia.

For nearly eighty years the Church of Christ has been a part of the Williamsburg landscape. From her humble beginnings in the house of an Army general to the present location on four acres on the east side, the Church of Christ has contributed significantly to the welfare of the local community. Substantial growth in recent years has resulted in our present membership of 170. I have been blessed to be the pulpit minister for this church since the fall of 1997, coming here from metropolitan Charlotte, North Carolina. We are led by a staff of four shepherds and nine deacons whose ministries are designed with the mission of the church in mind.

Despite the rising number of retired couples moving into this area, the average age of our members has decreased over the past few years. The median age is near fifty-five, a decline of two to four years over the past decade. Our leadership reflects this median age. The diversity within the church family echoes the diversity in the community as it is made up of most social, racial, and economic groupings. The style of worship in our church could best be described as "blended," mixing contemporary and traditional music. The church family is open to innovations that will increase the spiritual and numerical growth of the church. These innovations are met with little resistance as long as changes are understood to be biblical and expedient. This is the church of Christ in Williamsburg, Virginia.

Our diversity challenges our ministry efforts as we try to meet the needs of various groups. We want to avoid leaving any group of people out of the circle of importance, groups like older adults, the economically depressed, and even family leaders.

Ministering to Leaders

We believe husbands and fathers have been placed in a unique position within the family unit, namely, as the spiritual leaders. Even though it seems many men have abdicated this responsibility, it does not change the leadership role assigned to men in marriage and in the family. Since the beginning of time, God has leaned heavily upon the men in the homes to bring spiritual growth and stability to the family. Therefore one of our ministry goals is to encourage, challenge, and motivate men to assume their God-given responsibilities in the home and the church.

In our case the need to disciple became evident as we watched families in the church grow. God was sending us young families with fathers who wanted to be the spiritual leaders God intended them to be. A decade ago the number of adult males who participated in the church's ministries was extremely low. Today that number has increased substantially. Several years ago fewer than six men were involved in leading our worship time. Today nearly forty men are involved in this ministry. A decade ago we had no deacons to serve the church community. The work normally carried out by deacons was being done by the shepherds and minister, leaving them little time and energy for their primary responsibilities. There came a time when the words of Acts 6:4 rang clearly in the ears of our leadership: We "will give our attention to prayer and the ministry of the word." So we asked ourselves this simple question: "How can we achieve greater involvement and cooperation from the men in our church family?"

In my opinion there has never been a church that trusted God's grace and providence more than the Church of Christ in Williamsburg. We understood the biblical mandates of leadership, but we had allowed ourselves to become so involved in the daily administration of ministry that our priorities were in conflict. The words of Jesus (Luke 10:2) took on special meaning: "The harvest is plentiful, but the workers are few. Ask the Lord of the harvest, therefore, to send out workers into his harvest field." So we began to pray fervently for God to send us people with positive spiritual attitudes: workers, leaders, and servants. We prayed this prayer within our leadership group and in the public assembly. We prayed for people with enthusiasm, ideas, and a clear vision. God not only heard these desperate cries for help, he answered them with people. Lots of people. Gifted people.

Time to Evaluate

The next step we took involved an assessment of our church family. We knew one another by name, but we knew little about others' gifts, expectations, and dreams. We solicited the help of John Ellas from the Center for Church Growth in Houston, Texas, to lead us in an evaluation. The process took nearly six months and occupied a great deal of our time. Each member of our church family received a lengthy survey with detailed questions about his or her family's expectations and abilities. The responses to the questionnaire were compiled and evaluated by the center's professionals. Mr. Ellas spent a weekend with us detailing what he had discovered about our church family and suggested seven steps for revival within the church. We studied the seven suggestions carefully and felt that we could realistically accomplish five. Those five steps were put into practice during the next few months with great success and contributed largely to the involvement of our men. Most of us believe that without this evaluation, many of the needed changes would never have occurred.

One element in this second step was the establishment of a Sunday morning class for couples ages twenty to forty designed to help them meet the needs of their families. Many young husbands and fathers became an intricate part of this class, and the eventual success of the transition within the whole church was largely due to their participation. As the needs of these young families were being addressed, we began to see men stepping up to carry out responsibilities that had been left unattended. This served as a stimulus for the whole church family to become more involved.

The natural progression of this effort was to find ways to encourage male leadership in the family and church. We put forth a concentrated effort to discover men who were capable and willing to lead Bible study groups of all ages. Presently about fifty percent of our Sunday and Wednesday Bible class teachers are males who either work alone or with their wives. New adult Bible class teachers have been developed, giving our men a chance to grow as they prepare their lessons and become more involved in the lives of others in their own age group. This leadership ability has expanded into our children's ministry (Youth Adventures and Training for Worship). The youth group which had been led largely by one or two women has blossomed into an active group led by several adults, both male and female. Working together they have developed a youth ministry with great potential as they focus on spiritual growth, community service, and social interaction. Other areas of ministry have originated from this experiential work among our men and boys. Our educational, financial, and family growth ministries are all being led by men who are doing excellent work in these areas. Many of the ministries of the church are led by men and women working together in harmony, providing the additional benefit of making marriages and families stronger.

Meeting Needs

As we continued our evaluation, we realized many social needs of the men in our congregation were not being addressed. One of our first responses was to conduct a men's retreat at a local 4-H camp. Participation was minimal, but it was a springboard for other efforts. For several hours we discussed how we could become more effective leaders within the church. Within the past three years we've made a concentrated effort to engage men in social activities. These efforts have been accomplished through a program we call "Men's Night Out" where we gather at a local restaurant for dinner and fellowship. Some refer to these as our HBO (Helping Brothers Out) ministry. These are usually attended by more than half of our male members and have become an effective means of outreach to men who are unchurched. These informal gatherings are scheduled on an "as needed" basis. Another activity that has grown out of this effort is our "Sunday Afternoon Men's Fellowship." These gatherings are held following our Sunday morning activities and have become a highlight of our men's ministry. Each man is asked to prepare a "dish" of his own choosing without the help (except perhaps for oversight) of his wife, mother, or friend. Following some good-natured chiding about these culinary efforts, we have a time for some growth activities directed to Christian men and boys. These Sunday fellowships are led by alternating teams of two men and have been very successful. In addition, we plan recreational activities to which our men can invite their friends. We also host semi-annual golf outings arranged by one of our young men.

Often the strategies behind our men's ministry have surfaced as the ministry has grown. It is common to hear someone suggest a new idea for a men's gathering, and without exception the idea is given a green light. We believe in the value of variety when it comes to ministry. There is some good in continuing a successful program, but it is equally rewarding to alter a ministry to achieve renewed interest and greater success. Another unwritten strategy is that we will not become discouraged by a small number of participants. If one or two persons are helped by being together, we believe the time and energy spent are well worth it. We know that some men find it more relaxing to be part of a smaller number and will participate at a higher level when not threatened by a larger group. So whether two brothers share breakfast together at a fast food restaurant or thirty men chow down at a local buffet, we know someone will be helped.

Perseverance

We found it a challenge at times to get some of our men's ministries up and running. Because we had lacked an effective men's ministry for years, our men could not follow the example of previous generations. Our ladies had excelled way beyond what the men had accomplished. It took the initiative of a few men working together to grow this ministry. Christian men often hesitate to share their lives with other men. It doesn't seem like the manly thing to do! Women talk about their feelings, but men get grease on their hands from working on automobile engines This is a stigma nearly every church will face as it ventures into a ministry for and about men. The solution to this challenge is to cultivate an atmosphere among the men in the church that says, "This is important and we will not let it die!" Perseverance has its reward.

Our ministry to men continues to expand, becoming more of a vital part of our church's service and outreach. There is a very real sense in which we are limited only by our lack of imagination. If one person can dream it, a dozen can make it happen. Our goal is to see this ministry meet the needs of every man in our congregation, whether that man is single, married, or single again. Some of the basic needs men have that can and should be met by the local church include self-esteem, value as an individual, development of leadership skills, and personal spiritual growth. Our goal is to provide services that will help meet these needs and strengthen those eternally valuable Christian characteristics.

It may sound odd to say we have no concrete plans for this ministry, but it is true! We have a basic structure, but we also remain open to new ideas. Some of the ministry possibilities we are considering include automobile maintenance for single women and mothers, organized recreation for men and boys, camping trips, seminars on subjects that are of interest to men, and evangelistic outreach to men in the community. We strive to be flexible when it comes to meeting the needs of people. We do not go down a road with the idea that this is the right road and there will be no turning around or backing up. If we discover we are traveling the wrong road, we have no hesitancy about choosing a different path. We may have to make several adjustments in our journey before discovering the highway to success, but with God's help we will discover it.

Mentoring Younger Men

Another important goal of our men's ministry involves mentoring young men and boys who will assume leadership positions in coming years. We do not want to hand them the responsibility without the benefit of example. We understand the importance of mentoring relationships because most of our current leaders did not have such an advantage. In some ways this lack of mentoring retarded the growth and effectiveness of the church for many years. We would like to instill in very young man the desire to serve as an elder or deacon with a clear understanding of what these ministries require. With an ever-present preacher shortage, we would like to encourage our young men to consider the ministry of the local church. Another great need among churches is for effective music leadership. We would like to prepare young voices to lead others in praising God through singing. The list seems endless.

Given the present crises facing marriage and the family, we want to show young men how to become loving husbands and faithful fathers. With statistics rising each year reflecting an increase in single parent homes and homes without male influence, we believe such a ministry could do much to stem the tide of domestic violence and child neglect in our society today. The Bible teaches that this is the responsibility of the older men, and we take this charge seriously. Within every church family there are young boys who do not have the benefit of a loving father and these boys present a major ministry opportunity for men in the church.

The Church of Christ in Williamsburg, Virginia, strives to be sensitive to God's leadership when it comes to serving. We do not believe God has left his people alone in this world, but has given us the Word, his Holy Spirit, and each other to determine what our next steps will be. We've chosen not just to talk about such direction, but to be open to God's providential direction. A saying heard often around our church is, "Luck is for unbelievers; we believe in the power of God!" We know God is actively involved in our church because we have witnessed many examples of his intervention. I am confident that some are so afraid of giving God "too much" credit that he has received "very little!"

My advice to any smaller church that wants to unleash her potential would be to "step out of Jesus' way and let him build his church!" We are living stones used to build a spiritual house, but Christ will always remain the chief architect, cornerstone, and builder. One old country preacher used to say, "Jesus never said he wanted us to build his church. Neither did he say he would build our church. Jesus said that he would build his church!" I want to be a part of the process that continues this building project. God can do it without me, but I don't want him to do so! Do you?

Taking Action

Some of the action steps for such a ministry are not unlike other ministries. Building an effective men's ministry begins with complete dependence upon God. Pray. When one is involved in the work of God, he must depend on God's leadership and God will provide it. If we are sensitive to God's direction in men's ministry, we will see unparalleled spiritual growth in the family. Men will become better husbands and fathers. They will take on leadership roles within the church. Men will begin to look for ways to mentor their peers and younger men. It will be a sight to behold!

A second thing that needs to be done to make a men's ministry effective is to remove the chain that has kept some men tied down. Fearing that some might introduce innovations with which we are unfamiliar, some church leaders have become micro-managers. They want to know every detail about every decision. They want to be sure no one moves too quickly. They want to have their hands on every aspect of every ministry. A men's ministry will never succeed under such scrutiny. The leadership must wait for an end result before deciding the value and success of the ministry. A group of visionaries will give a man (or men) a dream and the freedom to turn the dream into reality. Not only does this relieve some of the leaders' burden, it increases the involvement of others in the process.

No pattern in the New Testament exists for this type of ministry, and anything that is not contradictory to divine truth is open for examination. It would be good for churches who are developing a men's ministry to seek the advice of churches who have succeeded in this area. The Internet can connect you to a growing number of churches with wonderful men's ministries. Sharing ideas your men have for this ministry is a great first step. That quiet little brother who never opens his mouth unless called upon may have some excellent ideas. Include as well the thoughts and ideas of those who are younger. Use your imagination and the imaginations of others to plan a ministry that will suit the needs of the local church.

Someone said, "Plan your work and then work your plan!" Many great ideas never get out of the discussion stage and therefore accomplish nothing. It can be discouraging for a group of people to have a workable plan for ministry that is never implemented. A few efforts left on the proverbial drawing board will soon douse any possible fire of success. If a ministry is to work, the time spent praying about it, working on it, and forming it is time well spent. Don't let a good work go undone because no one carried through with it. Remember, a ministry that is never completed is a ministry that may never be tried again.

Think about failure as only a bump in the road, not an insurmountable wall. We know the adages about trying again and again. In ministry those same truths are important because few efforts are completely successful the first time they are tried. Perseverance is the key to success. If you want your men's ministry to succeed, don't let it die. Keep it going regardless of the response the first time or two a meeting is called. Don't get discouraged because some you thought would surely be involved are not as eager as you are. Wait them out. Let them see the success of the ministry team and they will soon come around and become a part of the service.

Smaller churches can do big things. The success of the smaller church can be a welcome surprise even to its members, and will certainly be noticed by those on the outside looking in. Many smaller churches are humbly serving God without any notion of becoming a church that will impact a world larger than their own neighborhood. That's one reason I have loved working with smaller churches for the past 42 years. Most are unassuming and unpretentious. When asked to share their successes with a larger audience they quietly smile, tell their story, and go about discovering new ways to serve in their community. The Church of Christ in Williamsburg, Virginia, would make a very little splash in the ocean of church growth, but we are grateful for the small ripples that might help a sister congregation.

CHAPTER TEN

WOMEN'S MINISTRIES:
REACHING, TEACHING, AND MENTORING WOMEN

COLLEEN KING

D URING THE THIRD QUARTER OF THE 19TH CENTURY, following the Indian War of the 1850s, some of the Willamette Valley settlers retraced their steps on the Oregon Trail to settle in Umatilla County, northeast Oregon. By 1871 believers had banded together and were holding church services in area schoolhouses, and in the spring of 1873, Athena Christian Church was founded. Originally named the "Wildhorse Congregation," the church changed its name to Centerville Christian Church, and then later, after the renaming of the town from Centerville to Athena, the church changed its name again to Athena Christian Church (ACC).

Athena, Oregon, a farming community of 1,270 people, has a rich pioneer heritage of faith and dedication to God. Located at the foot of the Blue Mountains, this fertile region is the growing place for wheat, barley, peas, canola, garbanzo beans, and cattle. There are four churches in this small town, nine churches in the immediate area, all of which come together once a month to sing together and fellowship. Some of the churches provide community Bible studies and youth groups.

Our church building is 103 years old and has been well-maintained over the years. Our congregation represents all age groups. In the last five years our congregation has grown significantly, due to our leaders' dedication to bring a disciple-making process that focuses on making disciples who will make more disciples for generations to come. Sunday worship attendance averages 110 people and Sunday school 73, a significant increase over the last five years.

A Disciple-Making Approach

In February of 2001, several of our church leaders made a commitment to attend training provided by T-NET International, a global training network for disciple-making churches. Though I'm writing about women's ministries, I feel it is important to convey where our church stands on how we approach all ministry. From T-NET we learned that while most churches "believe" in making disciples, few are significantly succeeding in that role. According to a T-NET brochure:

- The average evangelical church wins less than two new converts a year per 100 attendees.
- Church members are no different in morals, ethics, and behavior than the unchurched.
- From a church survey of 6,000 church members, there was absolutely no correlation between length of church attendance and spiritual maturity.

T-NET's approach was to coach our entire church leadership team, not just the minister, through a proven training process lasting approximately 32 months. We were trained to:

- develop our own biblical definition of a disciple.
- train leaders.
- develop a ministry plan (or blueprint) to explain how we operate in ministry.
- develop ongoing multiplication of leaders through apprenticeship.
- improve the "feel" of our worship services, Sunday school time, small groups, and outreach events.

Since we began T-NET training in 2001, our worship service attendance has grown 21 percent, Sunday school 33 percent, and our giving has doubled.

How does women's ministry fit into this? As an intentional disciple-making church, we believe every ministry within our church family needs to be designed to reach out to the lost, provide sequential growth steps for everyone, provide a place for people to serve and use their spiritual gifts, and provide training to mentor subsequent generations. Built into this is a deep level of accountability for those who choose to step out in faith and let God train them to be disciples.

Early Stages of Ministry

I started at ACC as part-time secretary three months after our present minister arrived. A few years later I assumed the church janitor position and then my hours were expanded to full-time when I assumed the role of women's ministries coordinator.

The decision to add fifteen hours of additional staff time per week for a women's ministries coordinator resulted from a process that took about four months. Several women in the church (including me) had begun talking about designating someone in the church to coordinate our women's activities. We met together and prayed, seeking God's direction. I had always had a heart for ministering to women and have had many women friends in the church and community. I expressed my interest in the position.

The elders met and decided to contact church members to get feedback about creating a part-time, paid women's ministry position. After many phone calls, the elders offered the position to me. The next step was to gather the women together and talk about women's ministries. How would we do this? How would we get started?

We decided the first step would be to create a core team consisting of women who felt called to women's ministries. After two meetings we were able to articulate a mission statement for the core team. They agreed that before we could go forward with our women's ministries, they first had to understand their role as core team members. Our original core team mission statement was:

The core team's mission is to provide encouragement, safety, accountability, and direction for the women's ministry coordinator and for core team members while we accomplish the following:

(1) prayer support for each other

(2) accountability for each other

(3) research of successful women's ministry programs in other churches

(4) guidance for the coordinator

(5) planning support—to provide vision for short-term and long-range planning

(6) direction for women's ministries at Athena Christian Church with the goal of women mentoring women while keeping our focus on making and maturing disciples

The core team met again and chose a direction for women's ministries for the next six months. We agreed to postpone our long-range planning until we completed our research of other church's women's ministry programs and conducted a needs assessment of women in our church body.

For the next six months we focused on:

- Visiting women who were new to the church. These visits were designed to help us establish friendships. They were brief and documented.
- Visiting the saints. We visited those who already were church members. These visits were also documented.
- Planning outreach and fellowship events.

Launching the Program

This six-month plan was presented to the elders, and with their approval I officially began as women's ministries coordinator.

During this time I ordered two women's ministry books: *Women Reaching Women* by Chris Adams, and *Transformed Lives,* also by Chris Adams. In these books the author stressed prayer and Bible study as the foundation for women's ministry. Women need opportunities to grow in Christ and in the knowledge of God's Word. They need fellowship and a place to use their gifts in service. I felt confident we were on track.

At subsequent core team meetings we decided to continue with the activities from our original plan. Several gave reports on their research of other church's programs, but these churches were all large (over 1,000 members), and it was difficult to apply what they were doing to our smaller church family and community. We agreed to stay with the basics of women's ministries: Bible study, fellowship, and service.

We began a weekly fellowship time for the women of the church and community. The focus was outreach, as it is with all our events. We called it "Love 'n Lattes," a Thursday morning coffee time open to all women. We encouraged young moms to bring their little ones along.

Our church was now offering the following fellowship opportunities for women of the church and community:

- Community Bible Study (meets weekly and has joint leadership between our church and another local congregation)
- Ladies Birthday Lunch (monthly)
- Movie Night (about every two months)
- Ladies Day Out (about every three months)
- Love 'n Lattes (weekly)
- Retreat (annually)
- Ladies Christmas Breakfast (annually)
- Special events/speakers (whenever we can)

Charting Our Progress

After one year the core team met and reviewed our goals. The only goal we had not accomplished was to do a survey of the women in the church. I began to research surveys and questionnaires in some of my women's ministry books.

By this time I was doing a monthly report for the church board, keeping track of my activities and how I used my time. I reported the number of home visits I conducted, along with hospital visits, phone visits, and visits with women who came to the church office. Even though the office visits were informal, any contact with a woman was to be counted. In addition, I kept track of the activities I was involved in. During this time, something was happening inside me. Something uncomfortable. I was having trouble focusing and I began to feel overwhelmed.

I was beginning to feel the stress of my involvement in women's ministries. Where was the joy? I found myself feeling anxious about meeting new women who had started coming to the church. The dread was subtle, but it was there. How could this be? I felt tired much of the time and even made a doctor's appointment to make sure I was not ill. And worse, I kept all this from the core team. I had lapsed into fear without realizing it. I told myself I didn't want to bother them, afraid I would sound ungrateful and whiny. "This is not about me," I told myself, but the anxiety remained—confusing, considering women's ministries was something that had always made my heart sing. Now that I had the ministry I desired, was I going to start complaining and attempt to get out of my obligations?

When a woman would call the office, I would tally the call. When I would go to someone's home to visit, I would write it on my calendar. One week I made 15 home visits, tallying each one, but not remembering the purpose of the visits. I began to think in numbers instead of people. How many checks can I put on the list today? How many visits is enough? How many is too little? I knew I had gone into fear and people-pleasing, but I was unsure about how to get out. I wanted to do a good job but I began to feel like I was just going through the motions, and my heart was hiding in fear, hiding even from myself. My daily Bible study and prayer time was slipping and when I wrote in my journal, I felt the weight of all the obligations I was carrying in my life. My pain poured out onto paper as I wrote, but I felt very little relief.

Sharpening Our Focus

One day I asked a friend, someone not on the core team, to pray for me. She said she would. She came back to me a few weeks later with an answer. She felt as if God had told her I was doing too much, that I was carrying too many wounds to be in a leadership position, and that God had given her a vision of Jesus carrying a lamb around his shoulders. She said that was what Jesus wanted to do with me. He wanted me, not my activity. As hard as it was to hear this, deep inside my heart my spirit was in agreement.

As a result I met with the core team and we took a closer look at the coordinator's ministry description. My responsibilities included:

A. Purpose:
1. to reach women with the gospel.
2. to train women in the principles of making disciples.
3. to meet the needs of women.
4. to develop and oversee women's ministries.
B. Accountable to: the minister directly and to the elders through a monthly report form.
C. Ministry Requirements:
1. a member of ACC who is continuing to grow as Christ's disciple and has finished the second phase of T.E.A.M. Discipleship Training (Deeper Life Group) or agrees to join a Deeper Life Group as it becomes available.
2. in agreement with ACC's doctrinal statement and Blueprint for Ministry.
3. a role model of reaching out to women.
4. above reproach in her church and community (integrity and respect).
5. an equipper of women in ministry. She is not simply to do women's ministry, but to train women for ministry to women.
6. committed to working toward godly solutions when relationship difficulties arise.
7. submits to the oversight, protection, and direction of the elders as men who are spiritually responsible to God for the spiritual lives of every member of ACC.
8. consistent attendance in worship services and Sunday school.
9. willing to receive training in her area of ministry.
10. communicate to elders and minister through monthly report form.
11. time requirement: fifteen hours per week as paid staff of ACC.

Looking at this lengthy description, we realized we had built into our ministry a description of what a full-time women's minister would do. I came to realize I do not have a minister's heart. I am gifted in administration, mercy, and helps. The core team decided we needed to make revisions. As we examined the ministry description, another problem became apparent. We were trying to build the position around my abilities rather than what the church needed or what God called us to do. We realized that development of the ministry description must come before finding the right person for the job. I made a decision to step aside as coordinator of women's ministries, although I would remain on the core team.

We are now in the process of changing the ministry description to reflect the real needs of our congregation. We are assigning coordination responsibilities to the lead person rather than pastoral duties. To help us move into the next phase of our women's ministry development, the core team is working on a survey to determine the needs of the women in our church.

Learning from Our Mistakes

My biggest mistake was not going to the core team with my troubles. I was trying so hard to not make it "about me" that I made the situation worse, and more "about me" than ever before.

Another mistake occurred when we hired the coordinator first, then created the core team. We should have developed the core team first with a short description of the commitment level required and then developed the coordinator's ministry description before hiring a coordinator.

Even though we had a core team, women's ministries really wasn't core team directed. It didn't function as originally laid out, especially in prayer support and accountability. We lost half of the members within six months of our start up, which is common among new ministries. There will always be some who have an interest in the ministry, but have not really made the commitment to attend meetings, pray for the ministry, and actively participate. The core team is aptly named. Through their relationship with God and each other, they provide direction for the ministry. They are the "core."

We mistook accountability for numbers and record-keeping. It's important to keep good records, but it became a stumbling block for me.

We gave the leadership position to someone who was already responsible for other key ministries in the church. This was done to give me the equivalent of a full-time job in hours (the intention was good), but it put too much pressure on me. Smaller churches are often tempted to combine ministries to save resources. Sometime this works, sometimes it does not.

We built the women's ministries coordinator position around a person and her gifts instead of around what the church family needed.

What We're Doing Well

- Women's ministries is a part of the church and a part of our disciple-making process. We are dedicated to providing ways for women to grow in Christ and to teach them to mentor the next generation of disciples.
- We have changed the title of the women's ministries coordinator to women's activities coordinator, at least until we know what the church family wants and needs.
- Core team meetings have been changed from monthly to twice a month. This provides more oversight, more involvement, and more team prayer.
- We are reworking the coordinator's ministry description.
- We are revising our blueprint of ministry based on input from women in the church, and in keeping with our church's overall blueprint of ministry.
- We are working to determine the women's activity coordinator and core team's place in our church's organizational structure, where lines of authority and communication are defined.

Having learned that I must always go to the core team with everything that concerns me or women's ministries, I went to my core team when I was asked to contribute a chapter to this book, *Releasing the Power of the Smaller Church*. One of the core team members asked me two profound questions: "What is it we're doing that has power? What power are we releasing?"

And the answer came to me with the joy I had been missing. No matter how much any of us mess up, we are committed to each other. We stay in relationship and work hard to resolve conflict God's way while staying connected, just like God does with us. What could be more powerful than that?

We continue to explore the distinctions between a women's activities coordinator and a women's minister. We adopted and distributed a survey from Chris Adams' book, *Women Reaching Women*, to fit our needs. We want the ministry description to fit the real needs of our church family while fulfilling our commitment to reach the unchurched with the gospel through meaningful relationships and disciple making.

As we work to meet the needs of women in our church and community, we hold fast to each other and to God. I am thankful for the support I received from my church family. I am thankful that God saw my need and moved me out of a position that wasn't right for me, or wasn't meant for me at this time.

Some of our core team meetings have been challenging as we wrestle with our goals and philosophy of ministry. What good is ministry if we won't get along with each other? How strong is our testimony if we abandon each other? But how peaceful it is to be right with our sisters in Christ. Out of our relationship with God and each other comes service that blesses his name. My church family believes I am more important than anything I may do wrong. They believe that even when I make a mistake, I will learn from it. We can wrestle with an idea, even disagree, but not lose connection with each other. That is trust, and that is where Jesus creates deep obedience, deep passion for ministry, and deep connection with his people (John 13:35). That is the value Christ has placed on us. We just keep picking each other up, dusting each other off, and going forward.

CHAPTER ELEVEN

CONNECTING POINTS:
MEDIA, PUBLIC RELATIONS,
AND THE CHURCH'S IMAGE IN THE COMMUNITY

KEN TACKETT

I N 1988 I WAS TRANSFERRED from Chanute Air Force Base in Illinois to Malmstrom Air Force Base in Montana. The trip took us across the Northern Plains states, a place I was totally unaware of growing up in Oklahoma. Interstate 90 serves as the connector linking the east and west coasts in the North. As we drove across South Dakota, we saw the signs for Wall Drug (every mile and a half for 400 miles), the sign for Laura Ingalls Wilder's home (for the TV illiterate, she's the Little House on the Prairie girl), and the Corn Palace (a monumental palace constructed entirely out of corn). Aside from that, the 300 miles of Interstate 90 we drove through South Dakota didn't offer us much in the way of "Hey, I'd really like to live here!"

As the sun sank and darkness set in, what we didn't realize was that we were driving through some of the most beautiful scenery God has created on this earth. Located on the far western side of South Dakota are the Black Hills, named because of the deep green color of the pines. From a distance the green appears black, thus the "Black Hills." The Black Hills are home to some of the most scenic places in our great country. Mount Rushmore, the Crazy Horse Memorial, the Needles Highway, Custer State Park, and Devil's Tower are just a few of the sights to see. Our first trip to Montana took us through all this in the dead of night.

I've Been Called Where?

You can understand our hesitation when some 10 years later we were contacted and asked to come to South Dakota to help strengthen a smaller church. One member of the congregation kept emphasizing the beauty of the mountains and surrounding area, and all I could remember was 300 miles of prairie and a house made out of corn. But not wanting to be a "Jonah," we decided to make the trip to check it out.

What we found was a little slice of Heaven right in the middle of South Dakota. The town of Spearfish reminded us of Mayberry RFD. It was quaint and inviting with a population of around 7,000. Nestled in a valley bordered by mountains, many locals refer to it as the "Aspen of South Dakota."

The people were even more beautiful than the location. The small church was made up of about thirty to forty members, most of whom were young married couples with kids. They had been without a paid minister for several years but were willing and energetic to do whatever it took to see the kingdom grow in their community. One of the comments that solidified our decision to move to Spearfish came from the men of the congregation who asked, "We don't want you to come here and do everything for us, but we want you to teach us what we need to do." We moved to Spearfish three months later.

Our team hit the ground running in June of 1998. Within six months, our little group of thirty-five had grown to around sixty, and we were quickly running out of room in the small building the church owned. We were making plans and discussing an addition to the building when God introduced the next phase of our ministry.

Located just up the highway is the town of Belle Fourche. If you're a John Wayne fan, you'll recognize the name as the destination of his cattle drive in the movie *The Cowboys*. Belle Fourche is a ranch community of around 5,000 people. It's home to farmers, ranchers, and a host of professional rodeo cowboys. Separated by a mere ten miles, the difference in culture between the two communities is astounding.

Merging and Growing

Belle Fourche was also home to a smaller church of around twenty-five members. The church had recently lost its minister, who was largely supported by churches in the South. We began discussing with them their plans for the future, and before long we were talking about a merger.

The men of both congregations met one Sunday afternoon to discuss our options. We had been advised to spend plenty of time—months if necessary—discussing leadership issues, property issues, planning, ideology, theology, and of course, money. Instead, we met that afternoon, prayed together, and merged the next Sunday. We figured any problems along the way weren't too big for God to work out.

Our body of sixty-five or so was now in excess of ninety and our building was no longer adequate. We made plans to build a new building between the two communities and began the process of raising money. We bounced around from the Holiday Inn to an old Christian school, appropriately nicknamed "The Tomb" because of its dingy, grey cinder blocks and few windows. In March of 2002 we moved into our new building. Our group of ninety plus was now in excess of 120, and we couldn't wait to set up shop in our new location.

Since that time our body has seen continued growth. We now enjoy fellowship with more than 170 members (if we can ever get them all here at the same time). But more than the numbers, the spiritual growth that has occurred is far more staggering. We have seen the hand of God at work in the lives of people.

What Do You Mean, "Media"?

But now to the point of the chapter—the media, or more importantly, how the communities came to view us. I must admit, I was intrigued and yet somewhat daunted in the task of writing on this topic. Let me explain. As a means of replacing lost support from congregations in the South, I recently entered into a partnership with a brother from our body to form a media company in Spearfish. We produce a weekly television show, commercials, short and long format pieces, promotional DVDs, and video for the Web. When I was asked to write I thought, "Great! This is right up my alley."

It wasn't until later, when I began putting my thoughts together, that I realized that in our ministry in and around Spearfish and Belle Fourche, we hadn't even used the media, as most would define it. The traditional definition of media is "the means of mass communication (especially television, radio, newspapers, and the Internet) regarded collectively." The word *media* comes from the Latin plural of *medium*, which means "an agency or means of doing something." So for the purpose of this chapter my definition of *media* will be: "the way of doing something so the most people will hear about it and benefit from it."

In meeting with clients of our media company, the initial question that must always be answered is simple: What do you want people to know about you, your company, or your product? While the answer to that question may take on many forms for a business, for the body of Christ it is really quite simple. Our message is the same today as it was 2,000 years ago. We should want to communicate Christ and him crucified to all. That might seem simplistic, but when you boil it down to its most elemental part, Christ and him crucified is what remains.

Back to the business analogy for a moment. Once the question of what you want people to know is answered, you're left with the task of determining the best method or mode of informing your customer. It may be a commercial, an infomercial, or a promotional DVD. You then set about the task of producing it and getting the message out. The same process is true for the church, and it is the most critical and most overlooked aspect of many churches' ministries. We all, pretty much, would agree on the message. I'll throw this in for free: If your body can't come together on the message, the rest really doesn't matter. Gaining consensus on the mode or method of delivery of the message is altogether a different story.

The Method of Delivery

Part of the problem we face when we try to agree on the method of delivering the message is the plethora (the only word I learned from The Three Amigos) of ideas currently circulated along with the seemingly endless supply of church growth books that fill the racks of every corner Christian bookstore. Church leaders everywhere are reading books on growth, subscribing to Internet sites that promise the latest in innovation and technology, and attending every lecture within a thousand miles on the subject. These things are perfectly acceptable. However, if there's one lesson I've learned from living in South Dakota for the better part of 10 years, it's this: What works in Southern California probably won't work in South Dakota. What attracts people in Nashville doesn't attract people in South Dakota. What churches fight over in Oklahoma isn't what churches fight over in South Dakota. (By the way, our churches don't fight in South Dakota. And if you believe that, I've got some ocean-front property right next to Mount Rushmore I'd like to sell you.)

Asking the Right Questions

Maybe I can explain this another way. One of the hottest selling vehicles in the Dallas/Fort Worth Metroplex is the four-door, four-wheel drive, Chevrolet Suburban. You'll run out of fingers trying to count them as you drive around the city during the day. Consequently, the four-door, four-wheel drive, Suburban is also one of the hottest selling vehicles in South Dakota as well. However, the reason people in South Dakota are attracted to Suburbans is drastically different from the reason people in Dallas are attracted to them. In South Dakota, we actually use the four-wheel drive on our Suburbans most of the winter. My point is this: While the product (message) is the same, the media (the way of doing something so the most people will hear about it and benefit from it) will be different depending on where you are. So the hundred dollar question becomes: What is the right media for where I am today?

Unfortunately, this question leads to three more that must be answered before determining the appropriate media for your church. We will discuss all three individually, but here they are for now: (1) What are the demographics of the area in which I am ministering? (2) What are the cultures represented within those demographics? (3) What needs have presented themselves within these groups? If you can take the time to find the answers to these questions, any church of a thousand or any church of ten can effectively minister wherever it is located.

Whether you're selling a product or presenting the gospel of Christ, an understanding of the demographic profile of those you are attempting to reach is essential. *Demographics* is a big word used to describe the data you collect to help you understand your target audience. The following categories will give you an idea of what we are talking about.

Age

What are the ages of the audience you are trying to reach? Is your community primarily made up of retirees? Is there a large group of young married couples raising young children in your community? Do you have a college in your town and thus many young adults from 18–22? Determining the breakdown of ages within your area of influence is a must before determining the method of media you will employ.

Consider my mother. She is in her 70s and part of the World War II generation. She grew up without television, VCRs, and DVDs. I can still remember the first color television we had in our house. DVDs are foreign and she's still trying to figure them out. Add to that confusion the Internet and the Web. To my mother, a web is something a spider makes. I say all of this to make one important point. You may have the very best in Web site design for your church. You may have every announcement, ministry, prayer list, Christian link, worship schedule, and even a weekly note from the ministers posted on your site. But if the demographic makeup of your community consists primarily of people like my mother, people will never see it. Your message will die a slow death in cyberspace.

Now consider my son. He's 16 years old and much more proficient with technology than his father. He lives with a computer. His school issued laptops to all of their students. He can send text messages faster than I can type. He e-mails his assignments to his teachers rather than typing them as I had to do. Now if my demographic profile contains a considerable number of people from his generation, I had better include plenty of technology in any media I am considering.

Economic Status

Almost every local chamber of commerce can provide you with data about your community's economic situation. Basically what you're looking for is the total annual household income per family unit and how that compares to national averages. But don't get too wrapped up in national averages. You should know what is considered lower, middle, and upper income levels for your particular community. This is also important when considering the form your use of media takes. If your church is situated in an economically depressed area, dress alone (which is a form of media) can have a tremendous impact upon your message.

For example, if your church is in the custom or tradition of "dressing up" for worship, the message you may be sending is that in order to belong, you need to have nice clothes. If the majority of folks in your community don't know how to tie a Windsor, chances are neckties should be left at home. If no one in your congregation is in jeans and the majority of the community lives in jeans, you need to address the situation. Remember, everything we do as Christians is media. It all contributes to how we are perceived and thus how our message is received.

There are many other demographic statistics you can factor into your media style—single, married, divorced, single-parent family, black, white, or Hispanic. The most important aspect is that you take an honest look at the community you are in and then make the appropriate changes to convey your message in a way that will be well received by your community.

Culture

Many people seem to believe that since we all live in America, we all share the same basic culture. Nothing could be further from the truth. Every community in this nation has it's own unique culture in which the members of the body of Christ function.

In the North, especially the Dakotas, the vast majority of people are from Dutch and German descent. This cultural aspect alone took us a while to understand. Take for example church buildings. The current fad or trend in new church plants is the "coffee house" idea. Get some folks together at a coffee shop, have some java and scones, and sit around discussing the Bible. While in many communities (especially those with large numbers of young professionals and college students), this is by far the best method of communicating the message, in our community it would be disastrous.

To people of European descent, especially German descent, the existence of a church building is media in itself. These people have grown up in a culture that recognizes stability, structure, legitimacy, and piety in a building. While many people recognize a building as little more than a tool to be used, these people's culture sees a building as much more. We were not fully recognized by most members of our two communities until we completed our building. To the community, the building itself communicated a message—a message through which we communicate the Message.

Culture will also dictate worship styles (another form of media). Technology may not be the appropriate media for the culture in which you are working, but in another culture it might be a necessity. For a culture brought up on iPods, cell phones, and X-Box, technology is a welcome addition and even demanded by those whose learning styles are accustomed to flash. On the other hand, if the vast majority of my audience grew up sitting around a radio and have developed an auditory style of learning, songbooks with shaped notes are just what their culture expects. The true test of your media as it relates to worship is identifying all of the cultures represented and adjusting the media to communicate to those cultures.

Meeting Needs

The final question to be answered is one of needs. What are the needs of those to whom I am attempting to communicate? Snow tires don't sell well in Miami, Florida, and bathing suits are only available in South Dakota for a few weeks out of the year. In order to effectively plan and implement media that will communicate the message, we must understand the needs of those with whom we are communicating.

We've heard the quote: "People don't care how much you know until they know how much you care." For the past several years, in addition to my responsibilities as a minister, I have also handled the benevolence for our congregation. I had never dealt with this type of ministry before and went into it blind as a bat. While I didn't disburse cash unless absolutely necessary, I was quick to pay electric bills, fill up tanks of gas, and buy groceries on a regular basis. After a year or so into it, I noticed a distinct change in the phone calls. I was still getting the regular individual calls but was also now receiving calls from the local police department, the county jail, social services, the Salvation Army, and a house for battered women.

One afternoon after receiving a call from a police officer trying to find a place for a family to stay for the night, I asked him, "Why did you call me?" His reply would change the way I think about benevolence forever. He explained that beside the dispatcher's radio was a yellow sticky note with my phone number and a notation under it that read, "The church that helps people." You can't buy advertising like that! That message cannot be communicated through newspaper articles, Web site design, or television commercials. Again, everything we do as Christians is media, good or bad! We had unknowingly met a huge need in our community and thus the message of the love of Christ had been effectively communicated. We, as a body, could have told people how much we loved them, but the message wouldn't have been heard until we showed people we loved them.

Hopefully, you are interested in changing the way your community views your body. In order to accomplish this, honestly ask these three questions about your community:

(1) What do they look like? (Demographics)
(2) Where are they from? (Culture)
(3) What do they need? (Needs)

If you can answer these questions, the answers themselves will dictate the media needed to communicate the message of Jesus Christ to your community. Just remember the definition of media we started with: "the way of doing something so the most people will hear about it and benefit from it." After reading this I'm claiming editorial privilege to amend my last statement. While there are many valid forms of traditional media that can go a long way in communicating our message, the most fundamentally sound "media" we as members of the body of Christ need to employ is this: *We will do all things so that all peoples will hear the gospel of Jesus Christ and come to benefit from a relationship with him.*

CHAPTER TWELVE

BUILDINGS AND BUILDING PROGRAMS:
MAKING YOUR PRESENCE KNOWN

DAVID KESTER

I CAME UP WITH A GREAT SLOGAN for our congregation. The Church of Christ—We have a Place for You. Unfortunately, the slogan wasn't true. We did not have room for more people. Most Sundays we set up extra chairs, not because we were a large congregation but because we had a small building. One sad day a family told me, "We like this church but we are going to go someplace else. You don't have room for us." We had run out of room.

Our congregation meets in Cleveland, a town of 700 that is located in the prime agricultural area of south central Minnesota and is surrounded by dozens of lakes. The lake population helps Cleveland maintain an independent school district of between four and five hundred students. There are a few businesses in Cleveland, but most people find employment in neighboring towns.

The Church of Christ (one of three churches located within the city limits) has been a part of the community for more than 120 years. The church is respected throughout the community. We draw people from as far as thirty miles away and had a stable worship attendance of 90-100 for twenty-five years. We thought we might be able to grow if we had more room. In 2000 our congregation began to consider building a new church building. At first it seemed beyond our capabilities, but by the grace of God we were able to complete the task. I hope our story will encourage other smaller congregations to attempt things that seem beyond what they think possible.

Building a New Church Building Will Change Your Congregation

Building a new church building can be exciting, difficult, and frightening. If you build a new church building, your congregation will change. New leaders will emerge. The faith of your congregation will be stretched. People will give more generously than you ever thought possible. There will be fresh excitement in the church. You may also face conflict you had not faced before. Whatever happens, your congregation will change. Even positive change is difficult. We had to leave our comfort zone in order to build our church building.

Leaving the Comfort Zone

We had been comfortable for a long time. Every Sunday our sanctuary was full, often to overflowing. Our offerings covered our expenses. There was little extra money, but there was enough to pay the bills and support several mission efforts. We knew everyone. We liked each other. In a good year, we might have one or two families join us, enough to replace those who died or moved away. Things changed slowly in our congregation. We were comfortable with who we were. In that way, I think we were like many smaller, stable, rural churches.

Somewhere along the way we began to wonder if being comfortable was enough. Could God do something more with us and through us if we risked more for him? We knew God had not called us to be comfortable, but to be salt and light, to seek the lost, to be a transforming agent in the world. We were not sure we were living up to our calling. We wondered if our small, rundown, antiquated, stair-filled building was restricting our ministry. We wondered what would happen if we had a sanctuary that seated 200 instead of one that seated 100. What would happen if our building were handicap accessible? What would happen if we had off-street parking? Would a new worship facility allow us to reach more who were lost? Could we have a greater impact on our community and region? If a new building could make a difference, would we be willing to venture outside our comfort zone and build a new church building?

Where Will the Money Come From?

Those were not easy questions. Even if they had affirmative answers, we still had to answer the question, "Where will the money come from?" It seemed audacious for us, a congregation of 100 with a budget of only $70,000, to consider building a facility that would cost $850,000 when completed. (When we began we thought we might be able to construct what we needed for $500,000. Even that seemed like a huge amount of money to us.) We were forced to consider these options: (1) to continue to be what we had always been, or (2) to explore the possibility of doing something that would stretch us and our faith to the limit. With a degree of trepidation, we decided to follow the second path.

In the spring of 2000 we surveyed the congregation to see if our people were in favor of building a new church building. We knew the cost would deter some, so we wrote, "If money were not a concern, I would be in favor of building a new church building." Ninety percent of those who returned the survey agreed or strongly agreed that they would be in favor of building a new church building if money were not a concern. However, many were quick to remind us that money was a concern. In fact, money was the number one concern for more than half of those who completed the survey. How much money would a new building cost? How would we raise the needed funds? How much debt could we support? We liked the idea of having a new building. We knew we had not grown in our current facility for many years, and we wanted to grow. We wanted to make a bigger impact on our community and region. We thought having a new building might help us accomplish those things. However, we were not sure we had the resources necessary to build. It was exciting to dream of having a new church building. The thought of actually building and paying for it made us uncomfortable.

You Have to Start Someplace

At this point, many in our congregation still viewed building a new church building as nothing more than a pipe dream. I remember a key leader telling me, "David, we cannot do it. It is hard for us to pay the bills each month. Where will the money come from?" If we were to build a new building, we needed to do something to convince ourselves it was possible. The first concrete step we took was small but important. At a church board meeting in November of 2000, one of our deacons, a former bank president, said, "If we are ever going to build a new church, we have to raise some money." Then he said, "I move that on the second Sunday of every month we take two offerings with the second one going toward a new building." We discussed the proposal. We had never taken two offerings on a Sunday morning, but the motion carried unanimously.

At the beginning, contributions to the building fund seemed like a blind leap of faith. We began those offerings before we had plans, property, or a time line for building—before we had even been authorized to build. The money given was for the "If We Are Ever Able to Build" fund. With so few details in place, we were surprised to receive offerings of $1,000 or more each month. Evidently, some people in our congregation believed we could build a new building.

One Person Can Make a Difference

I was still somewhat skeptical. I wondered if we had the courage, the faith, and the will to tackle a project of this scope. Then one Sunday afternoon our church treasurer called me and said, "The new building offering was $21,000 this morning." I said, "You mean $2,100," which would have been our largest offering toward the new building to this point. Our treasurer said, "No, I mean $21,000." Then he told me that an elderly widow in our congregation had given $20,000 toward our new church building. I thought if one person was willing to give a gift like that, there might be others who were equally willing to give. That day I began to think it might be possible for us to build a new building. I started believing God really could do more than we can do. With him, nothing is impossible. Our building program ended up being more about God and his infinite resources than it ever was about us.

Take Another Step

However, with $48,000 in our building fund we were not quite ready to start building. So we formed a New Building Research and Feasibility

Committee (NBRFC) to explore the possibility of constructing a new building. It still seemed safer, and more comfortable for us to talk about research and feasibility than to make a commitment to build. Our research took two years. The committee toured dozens of church buildings and began putting together ideas of what our new building might look like. More and more people began talking about "when we build our new building" instead of "if we build a new building."

God Owns All the Land

As more people got on board with the idea of building, a new question arose. Not "Can we afford it?" but "Where will we build it?" Our current property was not adequate for a new building. We wondered if the availability and price of land would keep us from building. Could we even find a place in our small town to construct a building? Every time we asked, "Where will we build?" the chairperson of the NBRFC said, "Don't worry about the land." Then in an act of great generosity, he and his wife donated 3.25 prime acres of land on the corner of the two main highways that run through our town. It was not only a good location; it was the best location in our town for a new church building. I remembered what a building consultant had told me. "God owns all the land." Don't worry about the land.

Prepare People to Give

By 2003, with a place to construct a new building, the NBRFC's completion of a preliminary floor plan of approximately 8,000 square feet and some exterior sketches of a building, we had gone about as far as we could go without taking another major step. We had to embark on a major fundraising campaign to see if we could afford to build. We had never done a capital fund-raising campaign. We had never asked people to make pledges or commitments to giving. In fact, we seldom talked about money. We simply expected people to give what they could. We were uncomfortable with asking people to give sacrificially. To tell the truth, we were uncomfortable with asking people to give at all. We had to leave another area of comfort behind to embark on a fund-raising campaign.

By this time, we had nearly $85,000 in our building fund. We had determined that we would need at least another $290,000 to begin building. We adopted the slogan "Not equal gifts but equal sacrifice." We said we needed and would celebrate every gift from $1 to $10,000. We prepared to give a special Thanksgiving offering and make three-year pledges toward a new building.

After talking about our "Celebration of Sacrifice" offering for six months, we spent five weeks in intense preparation for the offering. During that time we read the entire New Testament together. We memorized five Scripture passages, none more important than these words from Matthew 17:20: "I tell you the truth, if you have faith as small as a mustard seed, you can say to this mountain, 'Move from here to there' and it will move. Nothing will be impossible for you." Then we prayed that God would give us the courage to bring the best gifts we could. We sent letters to those who attended our congregation as well as to interested friends. We asked for one-time financial gifts and three-year financial commitments as well as commitments of volunteer time and labor. When we mailed the letters, we wondered if November 23, 2003 would mark the beginning of the fulfillment of our dream or if it would mark its end. Our emotions ran the gamut from exuberant to scared-to-death. What would people give? We did not know.

I was concerned, so I prayed for a sign, something I rarely have done. I prayed, "Lord, please show me something that only you could do." Two days later the first response to our appeal arrived. It was from a nineteen-year-old college freshman. He pledged $3,600 to our building project, $100 a month for three years. A few days later we received another response. This one came from Texas. A check for $6,000 was enclosed as well as a three-year pledge. When I saw that gift I humbly prayed, "Thank you, Lord, for increasing my faith." I knew a nineteen-year-old freshman couldn't give $3,600. People who have only attended your congregation for a few months do not give $6,000. God was working. Now it was just a matter of waiting for November 23.

People Will Give More Than You Expect

Sunday, November 23, 2003 was a cold, wintry day. I had hoped our building would be packed, but only ninety-five attended that morning. Still, the service got off to a great start. We had said that it was more important to give your heart and life to Jesus than it was to give an offering toward a new building. In fact we said, "Do not give your money to this project until you have given your heart to Jesus." One young woman took that seriously and before we received the offering, she professed her faith in Jesus and was baptized. We knew that no matter what else happened that day, we had reason to celebrate.

Family groups, individuals, elderly people, and young children brought their offerings and commitments to the front of the sanctuary. When the offering was counted, $52,000 had been given in cash along with $257,000 in pledges to be given over the next three years. Fundraisers had told us we could expect gifts and pledges to be somewhere between one and two and a half times our annual budget. The gifts and pledges were more than four times our previous year's giving. When the totals were announced we celebrated. We are not a wealthy congregation. We often refer to ourselves as a bunch of ragamuffins. Who would have thought that ninety-five ragamuffins could give an offering like that? I was reminded of the words of King David from 1 Chronicles 29:14: "But who am I, and who are my people, that we should be able to give as generously as this?" We could not wait to tell our neighbors and friends what God had done.

When It Is Time to Build, Build!

After the offering was received, the building committee went into high gear. The chairperson of the committee announced our hope to break ground in the summer of 2005. His estimate turned out to be pessimistic. By February 2004, the building committee presented a preliminary floor plan to the congregation. The structure had grown from 8,000 square feet to 10,500 square feet An architectural firm was engaged and in April the congregation approved the floor plan for our new building. On May 30, 2004 the congregation voted overwhelmingly (ninety-seven percent) to authorize the building committee to accept bids and determine the groundbreaking date should the bids come in within the projected cost. The bids were in by early August and while I was on vacation, the board met and decided to proceed with building and financing a new church building. Our general contractor, a volunteer from our congregation, pushed to find excavators, concrete workers, and carpenters so we could begin building in time to beat the winter weather. He said, "This is the time to build. We will never find better prices." Ironically, he was the one who had told me four years before, "David, we cannot do it. We cannot afford it." God changes minds. Nine months after our Celebration of Sacrifice offering, we held our groundbreaking ceremony, August 29, 2004. It was time to build and we started building.

People Give More Than Money

By January 2005, the building was completely enclosed just in time to beat a bitter cold snap. From the middle of January until the building's completion, volunteers worked in the building almost every day. Our volunteer coordinator, relatively new to our congregation, spent virtually every day at the building for months and worked with and scheduled almost eighty volunteers. Nearly everyone in the congregation had some personal stake in the building process. Volunteers insulated and built walls, stained and hung cabinets, painted the interior of the building, installed casing, hung doors, built an attic storage area, installed hardwood floors, designed and made stained-glass windows, laid brick, built bookshelves, helped install tile, and did a host of other things too numerous to mention. This was our building. It belonged to all of us. We walked through the building and prayed. We wrote dozens of our favorite Scripture texts on the floors and doorframes. We wanted this building to be built on the strong foundation of God's Word, figuratively and literally.

The generosity of friends and strangers allowed us to a build a nicer building than we thought possible and allowed us to furnish it. To help contain costs, we had planned to use our old tables and chairs, along with our old sound system and appliances. We had even talked about painting some floors and waiting until we had the money to carpet them. We discussed framing in the education wing and finishing it ourselves. When we started building our faith was small, but we learned that faith the size of a mustard seed can move mountains and that nothing was impossible. An acquaintance agreed to design and make stained glass windows for our sanctuary on the condition that we would not pay her for doing so. One individual purchased new tables for our fellowship hall, another couple purchased tables for the classrooms, and another couple furnished the nursery. Money was given for new kitchen appliances and for seating in the sanctuary. Hardwood floors were donated and window trim given and installed.

God Will Do Things You Had Not Expected

Perhaps the most remarkable contribution we received came from an elderly stranger. He watched as the building was constructed and stopped a number of times looking for the minister. When we finally made connections he said, "I want to make a contribution toward carpeting." I explained that it might cost $500 to carpet a small classroom or maybe $2,500 for the carpet in the sanctuary. He nodded his head, took out his checkbook, and wrote a check for $12,000. That was the last time we saw him. God did things we had not anticipated.

The End of Building Is Only the Beginning

On June 5, 2005 we moved into our new church building. One hundred and ninety-five people attended that morning—exactly 100 more than had come together less than two years before at our Celebration of Sacrifice service. We have had more guests worship with us in the year and half we have been in our new building than we did during the ten previous years. Many of them now worship with us on a regular basis. Our worship attendance has increased by about forty percent.

Sometimes I ask people how they found us. Some say, "We watched your building go up. We were just waiting for it to be finished to come." One couple, when asked how they found us said, "Well, you are right there on the highway." Sitting at the intersection of the two main roads that go through our town, we could not have a better location. When we talked about doing some print advertising a while ago our treasurer said, "I think we just built a million dollar advertisement." It is good to be visible. One couple said, "We wanted to get married and we wanted to find a church and a church building. We saw yours and thought we would check it out." Another person said, "I wanted to come before but I couldn't climb the steps at your old building." Many say, "A friend invited me." It seems easier for us to invite friends than it used to be. We have space for guests in our building, and we have a building we are proud of. Our new building has attracted many people. We keep reminding ourselves that while a new building may attract guests, it will be the church (Christ's body) that keeps them coming back. The building is a tool; we, God's people, are still called to do the work.

We wondered what would happen if we had a sanctuary that seated 200 instead of 100; what would happen if we were handicap accessible; what would happen if we had off-street parking. We wondered if we could reach more people for the Lord and have a bigger impact on our community. We found out. We are reaching more people and are having a greater impact in our community. We also found that building a new building has had an impact on us. We are not quite as comfortable as we used to be; nor are we quite as worried about being comfortable. Our faith has grown, and we are wondering what God might have in store for us next.

If You're Thinking About Building . . .

(1) Take time to get key people on board with the project before you begin, even if it means going slower than you desire.

(2) Put into place a clearly defined decision-making process. Decide which decisions need to be made by the entire congregation, which decisions can be made by the church board or the building committee, which decisions are left up to the discretion of the general contractor, and then decide if there are other individuals who will be granted decision-making authority. Clarifying and streamlining the decision-making process will help your project go more smoothly and will eliminate confusion.

(3) Do not allow the building of a church building to take the place of

building a church. Protect your minister from excessive involvement in the building process.

(4) Use the gifts and talents of those in your congregation. You will be surprised at the abilities people in your church possess.

Getting Started . . .

(1) Begin a building fund, even if you have not yet set a time line for new construction. The only regret you will ever have in beginning a building fund is that you did not begin it sooner.

(2) Clearly define the reasons, importance, and goals for building. Share as much information with your congregation in as many ways as you can. We had hoped to have 100 percent support of the congregation for our building program and determined we would not proceed with less than eighty-five percent approval.

(3) Determine what you need in a building. Consult Sunday school teachers, worship leaders, nursery workers, kitchen workers, and other key individuals as you consider the floor plan and what to include in the building. The more information you gather, the easier it will be for an architect to design a building that meets your needs.

(4) Conduct a capital fundraising campaign. We did our own research and our own campaign. You may decide to use one of the many professional fundraising groups available.

(5) Find and acquire land. Remember God owns all the land.

(6) Hire an architectural firm that has experience in designing church buildings and one that is opening to working with you.

(7) Secure a general contractor or project supervisor. It is important to have someone on site as much as possible.

(8) Solicit and accept bids.

(9) Then, if everything converges, build!

CHAPTER THIRTEEN

ENCOURAGING WORDS FOR SMALLER CHURCHES

SHAWN MCMULLEN

I HOPE YOU'VE FOUND THE CHAPTERS IN THIS BOOK challenging and helpful. I hope they have helped you see the tremendous potential for ministry that exists in the church you serve. And I hope you're committed to helping your church tap into its God-given power to change lives and transform your community. So before we conclude this journey, let me share a few final thoughts I hope will encourage you for the work that lies ahead.

A Paradigm Shift

Think of a paradigm as a philosophical framework. As leaders and volunteers in smaller churches, our paradigms are ways of thinking about and doing ministry. Perhaps one important step for many of us in smaller churches is to change the paradigm from which we operate.

Those who serve the Lord in smaller churches are often tempted to think "small," focusing on obstacles instead of possibilities, limits rather than potential. So let me suggest a paradigm shift. Let's not think in terms of size or resources. Let's not worry whether our church will ever become a large church. In fact, rather than think about becoming a "mega-church," think about having a "mega-impact" on your community. Focus on what your church can do—right where it is—to change the spiritual landscape of the surrounding neighborhoods.

What can your church do today to touch the lives of the people who live near your building? Let me offer a few suggestions.

Make a Long-Term Commitment

I was in a meeting with several church leaders recently (leaders of smaller and larger congregations) when we began talking about some of the positive things that have occurred in our ministries in the last several years. Midway through our conversation someone spoke up. "Listening to the stories we're telling around the table, it seems like the seventh year in ministry became a turning point for many of us." Most agreed. I'm sure this isn't a hard and fast rule, but my colleague's observation made sense. For many leaders and volunteers in ministry, real growth comes not immediately, but after years of diligent effort that have paved the way for growth.

Sadly, many leaders and volunteers in smaller churches give up, slip into neutral, or change churches before the results of their efforts—and God's blessings—are realized. This often leads to a discouraging cycle where committed Christian workers serve in one location for a few years, leave to serve in another location for a few more years, and so on—never staying long enough to see the rewards of a long-term ministry.

My advice to preachers, elders, deacons, Sunday school teachers, youth workers, and other servants in smaller churches is this: Stay put. Covenant together with others in your congregation to endure the difficulties, help one another through the rough times, and simply hang in there long enough to see the results of your efforts. And when you do, you can thank God and bask together in the success he gives.

Think Outside the Box

When I say "Think outside the box," I don't want you to think about personal creativity and ingenuity—at least not at the moment. Instead, think of the word *box* as a metaphor for the building where you worship. If you want your smaller church to have an impact on your community, think beyond the walls of your building.

Some leaders and volunteers in smaller churches feel insecure about themselves and their congregations (often because they compare themselves to larger churches—something I hope we have learned never again to do!). This insecurity leads them to huddle together for support and protection, like the children in the often-cited study who huddled in the center of the school grounds when their playground fence was removed. When this sentiment prevails in a smaller church, people resign themselves to attending their own services and fellowshiping exclusively with one another. This provides a certain level of comfort, but it does little to transform the community. The longer a church remains in this situation, the more difficult it becomes to think outside the box.

Have you ever visited a church like this? They may think of themselves as a friendly church. In fact, they may refer to their friendliness on the sign out front and on the cover of the Sunday bulletin. But in the end they are friendly only to one another. Visitors feel left out and seldom return. People in the community know little about the congregation. They're not antagonistic toward the church; they're just ambivalent.

If you're willing, ask yourself this question about the church you lead or serve. "Do most of our programs and activities center around our own people, or do we deliberately engage in ministries that focus on people outside our four walls? Your answer may be a good indicator of whether or not your church is thinking outside the box.

Not long ago the church I serve decided to do something special for the communities that surround our church building. The town where our building is located had no fall community festival as did most every other surrounding town. So we picked a date, formed a committee, and began to plan the first annual Milan Fall Family Festival.

We advertised several weeks in advance in our local paper. We rented equipment to make cotton candy, snow cones, popcorn, and hotdogs. We provided barbeque, ham and beans, coffee, hot chocolate, and soft drinks. A group of our adults and teens built and supervised a number of festival games for children complete with prizes (everyone was a winner, of course!). We rented an inflatable jumping gym and roped off a large area of our lawn where kids could sit inside local emergency vehicles and tractor-trailer rigs. We invited local law enforcement agents who offered the "Identa-kid" fingerprint program to families. We gave away gifts throughout the day, staged a cake walk every 30 minutes, conducted an apple recipe bake-off with prizes, and provided a concert by a local Christian bluegrass band. We gave away pens, refrigerator magnets, and information about our church to every guest. Everything we provided was free, a concept that was well received in our community even though it took some people a while to believe it.

The folks in our smaller church went all out to make our Fall Family Festival a success. And it was. We estimated at least 500 community members attended the event and learned about our church. Several new families began attending as a result, and all because our smaller church was willing to think outside the box.

How can your church make itself known to your community?

Be Yourself

Just before David entered the battlefield to face the giant Goliath, the Bible tells us Saul placed his own tunic on David and fitted him with armor for his protection. David tried walking around in the armor, but soon realized it would be more of a hindrance than a help. "I cannot go in these," he said to Saul, "because I am not used to them" (1 Samuel 17:38, 39). So David removed the armor Saul had given him and went to face Goliath as he had faced the lion and the bear that attacked his sheep, wearing only the clothing of a shepherd.

It seems logical that young David would refuse to wear the tunic and armor of a mighty man like Saul. They couldn't possible have fit him and they clearly weren't comfortable. There's a lesson here for those of us who lead and serve smaller churches. We'll hear about many programs that work well in larger congregations—churches with more staff members, more programs, and more resources. Some of these ideas may work in our situations, but many will not and we shouldn't force them to fit us. Instead we should do what David did—go into battle as God has equipped us, trusting him to make up for whatever we may lack.

Smaller churches shouldn't try to be larger than they really are. That's not to say we shouldn't dream big dreams and plan big plans, but we must think and act realistically in order to do ministry effectively.

Use Your Assets

I mentioned in the first chapter of this book that smaller churches naturally have smaller talent pools from which to draw. That's true enough, but at the same time we may be surprised at the amount of untapped talent that resides in many smaller churches. Do you know how many teens and adults in your smaller church have musical talent? Why not find out and use their talents individually or collectively in your worship services? Do some of the folks in your smaller church have jobs that require them to lead, manage, or administrate? Why not tap into that talent to plan and organize ministries? Do you have a few folks to whom people naturally go when they're troubled? Why not get them some training and help them develop a counseling ministry in your church? Do the children and teens in your church naturally gravitate to certain adults? Why not plug those adults into children's or youth ministry?

My father-in-law, Herb Bleakney, worked for decades in a Pennsylvania steel mill. That was his day job. But in the evenings and on weekends, he was part of an elite group of men in his smaller church who took upon themselves the task of discipling the young people in their congregation. The men who helped him worked full-time jobs and had families. While my wife and her siblings were in their teen years, these men poured themselves into the lives of the church's youth. They planned activities, took them on distant trips to youth events, and gave up weeks of vacation time to be with them in summer church camp.

Through the efforts of these three men and the support of the church, 22 kids from their youth group enrolled in Christian colleges during that period. Two became missionaries to Jamaica. One served with her husband on a Bible translation team in Papua, New Guinea. One entered the youth ministry and now teaches at a Christian university. Another has spent the last quarter of a century with her husband equipping and encouraging church leaders in a Bible college in the Northwest. One serves a Bible college in ministry to its alumni. One is part of a mission organization that trains and sends mission teams around the world. Another married me (and for that I am most grateful). Many others from this youth group are serving Christ today in their local churches and in the workforce.

Outside of an occasional pat on the back or a word from a grateful parent, these heroes of the faith received little recognition for their work.

But then again, they weren't seeking it. They were simply serving Christ the best way they could.

The world will never know the extent of the impact these men made for the gospel of Christ. But I caught a glimpse of their impact when my father-in-law was killed in an automobile accident. The church building was packed for his memorial service. One of the young men he discipled, now the alumni director of a Christian college, stood before the crowd and told how Herb had challenged him to return to Bible college and continue his preparation for the ministry even though he was making other plans. He is in the ministry today largely because of my father-in-law's influence. The missionary couple in Jamaica tried unsuccessfully to find a flight to the states so they could attend his funeral. When they realized they couldn't return home in time, they faxed a letter to be read during his memorial service thanking God for Herb's influence on their lives. In the days that followed the "kids" from this youth group called, wrote, or stopped by to pay tribute to Herb and his coworkers for the time they invested in their lives.

All this took place years ago in a smaller church where a few ordinary but faithful men with no formal training took it upon themselves to disciple the church's youth.

Their examples inspire and encourage me. And they give me great hope for the church I serve. I'm the only paid staff person in our church, but we have vibrant children's and youth ministries because we have a number of godly adults in our congregation who are passionate about helping kids grow up into Christ. We didn't find them; they found us. We simply prayed earnestly that God would raise up faithful and godly adults within our church and give them a passion for youth ministry. And he did.

Who knows what kind of ministry potential exists among the people in the church you lead and serve?

Take the Lead

Following his famous battle with Midian, the Old Testament judge Gideon ruled Israel for forty years. He married many wives and had seventy sons. Another son, Abimelech, was born to him by a concubine.

When Gideon died, Abimelech sought support for a political coup from his relatives in Shechem. The citizens of Shechem gave Abimelech money from the treasury of a pagan god, and with it he hired a group of mercenaries whom he led back to his father's home in Ophrah to kill his seventy brothers. Only the youngest, Jotham, escaped the slaughter.

With his political competition eliminated, Abimelech met with the citizens of Shechem in Beth Millo to be crowned king. When Jotham heard about it, he climbed to the top of Mount Gerizim and addressed the crowd in a parable, warning them not to choose such a poor leader (Judges 9:8-15):

> One day the trees went out to anoint a king for themselves. They said to the olive tree, "Be our king." But the olive tree answered, "Should I give up my oil, by which both gods and men are honored, to hold sway over the trees?" Next, the trees said to the fig tree, "Come and be our king." But the fig tree replied, "Should I give up my fruit, so good and sweet, to hold sway over the trees?" Then the trees said to the vine, "Come and be our king." But the vine answered, "Should I give up my wine, which cheers both gods and men, to hold sway over the trees?" Finally all the trees said to the thornbush, "Come and be our king." The thornbush said to the trees, "If you really want to anoint me king over you, come and take refuge in my shade; but if not, then let fire come out of the thornbush and consume the cedars of Lebanon!"

The final verses of Judges 9 show that Jotham's prophetic warning rang true. Soon after, Abimelech was killed and the citizens of Shechem were punished.

Jotham's parable contains an important truth for the smaller church. We might think of it as the "leadership by default" principle. When capable people refuse to lead, leadership invariably falls to those who are less capable. People want to be led. In fact, the need to follow is so strong in many people that they will accept an unqualified leader rather than do without.

When this happens in the church, everything suffers—outreach, discipleship, vision, planning, organization. How can we protect the church from the leadership by default principle? To begin, if you're capable, perhaps you ought to lead. You know leadership can be difficult and thankless. You may not like the limelight. You may be smarting from negative reactions to your last attempt at leading. You may have become discouraged in your efforts to lead and walked away saying, "I don't need this!" But if you sense God pressing you into leadership, and if those around you confirm your ability to lead, shouldn't you lead?

Smaller churches need leaders in every area of ministry. Leaders who cast vision for growth, and leaders who cast actors for the Christmas program. Leaders who change direction, and leaders who change diapers. Leaders who direct building programs, and leaders who direct Vacation Bible School.

Don't wait to be asked. If you don't lead, who will?

May God richly bless your efforts to release the power of the church you serve.

e s c n
energizing smaller churches network

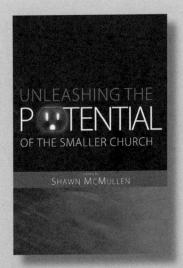